TRUE CHRISTIANITY

Books by John W. Whitehead

The Separation Illusion

Schools on Fire (with Jon T. Barton)

The New Tyranny

The Second American Revolution

The Stealing of America

The Freedom of Religious Expression in Public Universities and High Schools

Home Education and Constitutional Liberties (with Wendell R. Bird)

The Right to Picket and the Freedom of Public Discourse

Parents' Rights

The End of Man

An American Dream

True Christianity

TRUE CHRISTIANITY

John W. Whitehead

CROSSWAY BOOKS • WESTCHESTER, ILLINOIS
A Division of Good News Publishers

First printing, 1989

Back cover photo: Steve Heyl

Printed in the United States of America

Library of Congress Catalog Card Number 86-70288

ISBN 0-89107-399-X

Biblical quotations
are taken from *New American Standard Bible,*
copyright © 1960, 1962, 1963, 1968, 1971
by the Lockman Foundation,
La Habra, California.

To
my wife, Carol,
who really knows me, but sticks with me,
and to
my children, Jayson, Jonathan,
Elisabeth, Joel and Joshua (Noodles),
who keep me from taking life too seriously

Contents

ACKNOWLEDGMENTS

I would like to express my appreciation to Carol White-head for her proofreading of the galleys, astute suggestions and typing. The work of Mae Heitz and Todd Tuell on the bibliography was helpful. Thanks to Sally Mason for typing the words. I appreciate the support and assistance of Lane Dennis at Crossway Books. Also helpful were the suggestions of Michael Patrick, F. Tayton Dencer, Becky Beane and David French. Without these and others, I would not have been able to write this book.

TRUE CHRISTIANITY

PART ONE

THE HUMAN DILEMMA

Storm warnings, portents, hints of catastrophe haunt our times.

—Christopher Lasch[1]

The Titanic sails at dawn.

—Bob Dylan

They're talkin' about a revolution
It sounds like a whisper
While they're standing in the welfare lines
Crying at the doorsteps of those armies of salvation.

—Tracy Chapman

O n December 14, 1937, the Japanese high command ordered some fifty thousand troops to attack the Chinese city of Nanking and kill everyone in it. The invaders easily took the city and used the helpless citizenry for bayonet and machine-gun practice; they raped, burned, and dismembered others, including the unborn. Japanese officers held competitions to see who could behead the most children with one sweep of a samurai sword. The conquerors murdered over forty-two thousand people.[2]

At about the same time, Adolf Hitler's National Socialist *Reich* was in the process of exterminating millions of Jews. Joseph Stalin outdid the atrocities of both Hitler and the Japanese. Former Moscow correspondent Harrison Salisbury describes the scene as

> a whole continent of terror. . . . Compared with those who brought about the hundreds of thousands of executions and the millions of deaths in the Soviet terror system, the Czars seem almost benign. . . . Our minds boggle at the thought of a systematized, routine evil, under which three or four or more million men and women were sentenced each year to forced labor and eternal exile—and in a manner so casual that the prisoners often were not even told what their sentences were.[3]

More recently, Pol Pot and his Marxist-Leninist Khmer Rouge forces systematically slaughtered some two million of their own countrymen in Cambodia. In terms of the percentage of the population, it was the worst case of genocide in modern times.[4] One could go on to body counts in Uganda, Biafra, or Guyana, but it is undeniable to all but the willfully blind that the twentieth century has been one of tyranny and genocide. The optimism of the last century seems to have been shattered and the question remains: why has all this happened?

Nobel Prize winner Aleksandr Solzhenitsyn, one of the noblest and most courageous men of our time, put it this way:

Over a half century ago, while I was still a child, I recall hearing a number of old people offer the following explanation for the great disasters that had befallen Russia: "Men have forgotten God; that's why all this has happened."

Since then I have spent well-nigh 50 years working on the history of our revolution; in the process I have read hundreds of books, collected hundreds of personal testimonies, and have already contributed eight volumes of my own toward the effort of clearing away the rubble left by that upheaval. But if I were asked today to formulate as concisely as possible the main cause of the ruinous revolution that swallowed up some 60 million of our people, I could not put it more accurately than to repeat: "Men have forgotten God; that's why all this has happened."[5]

A Voluntary Darkness

Christians who believe in an historical Fall still find these mass atrocities horrifying, but they know what makes them possible: the reality of evil and the rejection of God. Unless they are moved by the Holy Spirit, people have a natural distaste for God. In fact, even though much of it may be unconscious, people literally hate God. They are alienated from their Creator, and hence from their fellow human beings as well. The proper term for it is sin. Christians, like the Apostle Paul, should know full well that sin affects every part of their nature.

Unfortunately, during the last two centuries there has been an erosion of faith in God. There has also been an erosion of Christian beliefs such as the sanctity of human life, in the Judeo-Christian ethic in general, and even in a belief in the existence of evil.

The rationalist movement, materialistic philosophies, Darwinism, scientific determinism, along with various militant political evangels such as Marxism, became the new orthodoxies. Ironically, though all these regarded man as an animal, a highly developed ape, one dogma they all shared was the essential *goodness* of man. For the new orthodoxies, evil was social, not personal, and was caused by the effects of society and the environment.

The secular vision often holds forth science and technology as salvation, but it should be apparent by now that neither is capable of saving us. Science cannot answer the mysteries of life, and technology is only a tool. This tool can be beneficial, but can also be used by sinful human beings to wreak massive suffering.

For example, it is easier to drop bombs from high altitudes than to look the victims in the eye. And technology provides the torturer with a spectacular variety of instruments to inflict pain and misery.

Psychoanalytic pioneer C. G. Jung traced many of his patients' problems to the loss of their religious beliefs.[6] In addition, Jung noted:

> It seems to me that, side by side with the decline of religious life, the neuroses grow noticeably more frequent . . . the mental state of European man shows an alarming lack of balance. We are living undeniably in a period of the greatest restlessness, nervous tension, confusion and disorientation of outlook.[7]

What applies to the individual also applies to society. A society and culture that have lost their faith will also be confused and disoriented.

The struggle for ideas and beliefs is always important

but becomes critical in times of flux and upheaval. Ideas and beliefs always have consequences, for the individual and for society. As history shows, someone or some group will always step into the vacuum and take control. Pre-1917 Russia and pre-National Socialist Germany are notable examples. The consequences are still being worked out, and the victims continue to pile up.

When God is denied, so is evil. As another Russian, Fyodor Dostoyevsky, put it, if there is no God, then all things are permitted. Likewise, those who believe God to be unimportant also tend to regard human beings as unimportant. Hence, the awful developments described above become explicable by their own materialist logic.

The Secular Monolith

While the kind of upheavals described by Salisbury and Solzhenitsyn may not constitute a present danger for contemporary American Christians, no one should be complacent. The ideas that caused those upheavals are still on the march in this century and gaining adherents everywhere, even within the church. The damage they cause does not always take the same form. But the end result is often the same: death on a massive scale.

Abortion

Abortion is violence, the spilling of innocent blood, and therefore a violation of the sanctity of human life. Tragically, abortion is now the most popular form of killing in America, if not the world. Millions of innocent and helpless lives have been snuffed out by abortion since the *Roe v. Wade* decision of 1973. This ongoing holocaust is a direct result of the devaluation of human life traceable to the loss of the Christian ethic, which honored the Creator and those created in His image.

The secular ethic views unborn and "unwanted" children as protoplasmic rubbish or "fetal tissue," to be used in medical experiments conducted with both animals and people.[8] As C. S. Lewis noted, he would not do "to minerals and vegetables what modern science now threatens to do to man himself."[9]

While this book is not a treatise on abortion, a few points need to be made. It is tragic that all true Christians do not actively oppose abortion. The proponents of abortion regard the practice as a method of "population control," and it is safe to say that in an increasingly secular age, it is within the realm of possibility that religious people in general and Christians in particular could eventually be regarded as a part of population in need of "control."

In addition, the "right to die" movement aims to delegate questions of life and death to medical professionals. Abortion is the slippery slope leading to infanticide (the killing of children) and euthanasia (the killing of adults). In the future, doctors or even government officials could well be making decisions on who lives and dies. In some cases, they do so now.

The sanctity of human life touches the very nature of man's existence. If not dealt with effectively, it spells the death of a nation. It will result in the death of humanity as we presently know it. And one should make no mistake about it: the right to life is the most basic of all rights. Hence, a country that does not protect human life will in the end protect no rights at all.

Pornography

Sex and power are the only forms of mysticism a secular society can offer, and American society is currently sex-crazed. The easy access to pornography in this country is a display of contempt for religion, the family, and the human being in general.

Pornography reduces people to sex objects. It portrays women, in particular, more as sex objects than human beings. It reduces sex from an act of love to a source of immediate gratification and eventually a form of manipulation.

A jaded populace is increasingly seeking to use children as sex objects. Intimations of this may be seen in advertising, where scantily clad twelve-year-old girls are used as models. And in one ad for wristwatches, young girls are sometimes shown in sexual situations with older men.

More seriously, hard-core pornographers seek children for use in "underground" magazines and films. In similar style, older homosexuals seek liaisons with young male prostitutes, sometimes known as "chickens." However, the ultimate end of pornography is not sex but violence, and movie producers have started to offer the real thing.

There is currently an underground trade in "snuff films," in which women are brutally killed and dismembered on film. Such depraved developments do not bode well for the future of Western civilization.

Decline of the Family

From time immemorial, the family has been the basic human institution, and the family, not the individual, is the fundamental unit of society.

In free societies, the family serves as a buffer zone between the individual and the state. The family takes care of its own members and also possesses property. Possession of property has historically been an important factor in reducing authoritarian tendencies in politicians and controlling civic government. This is why those who articulated the basic political philosophy upon which America functions held that the right of the individual to possess property is sacrosanct.

However, modern Americans are increasingly becoming propertyless. Those who claim to "own" homes are in reality renting them from mortgage companies. Instead of being in the hands of the people, property is more and more in the hands of banking firms and, of course, the state.

The more the family concedes to outside forces, the more the buffer zone between the individual and the state dissipates. The individual then stands naked against raw state power in what has become an atomistic society. This is very much the condition of the Iron Curtain countries, where the totalitarian state assumes the role as the overarching "family." More than a few Western politicians regard the state in this way.

American society is in many ways anti-family and anti-parent. Many of the major American institutions are opposed to traditional family structures. It may be that those who take these stances were reared in broken families or have never seen a real family operate. They thus tend to denigrate the family and do not ascribe much importance to it.

This is unfortunate because the family is where children learn the values they will carry with them through life. It is where they should learn to operate in a democratic society. If a society is composed of malfunctioning families, children will possess a muddled view of reality. The consequences of family breakup are all too obvious.

Denial of Rights

In his book *The Secular City*,[10] Harvey Cox noted that secular*ism* is a dangerous ideology because it tends to use the organs of the state to exclude all other viewpoints. It is not satisfied with being a dominant viewpoint, but seeks to be the *only* viewpoint. Secularism establishes a closed system. In practice, secularism leads to the stifling of religious speech and the forced eradication of free religious expression.

The Eradication of Symbols

For example, over the past several decades religious symbols have been systematically removed from public places. Every year there are battles over crosses and nativity scenes. This is also true of other traditional religious holidays as well. In one instance, Chicago city officials rearranged two crosses made from lilies at Easter flower shows after the American Civil Liberties Union objected that the displays promoted religion on public property.[11]

There have also been attacks on religious symbols in public parks and on public buildings. Even traditional street preaching has come under attack. In fact, there are an increasing number of cases in which street preachers have been arrested and brought to trial.[12] This kind of action is a relatively new development in American history.

The Public Schools

The First Amendment to the Constitution states that "Congress shall make no law respecting an establishment of religion, or prohibiting the free exercise thereof." This did not mean, as secularists contend, that religion was to be barred from public life. Rather, the Framers understood it to mean that the government was forbidden to establish an *official* religion, as was the practice of many European countries. It also meant that the government could not give preference to one religion or church over another. The lack of an official state church was believed, correctly, to bolster the free exercise of religion by all citizens. (In many European countries, groups who dissented from the official church were persecuted or restricted in their activities and pursuits.) In other words, the "No Establishment Clause" was designed to serve the "Free Exercise Clause." But although they forbade an official church, none of the Framers believed that religion was to be barred from public life.

Contrary to popular misconception, the phrase "separation of church and state" does not appear in the Constitution of the United States, but is found in the writings of Thomas Jefferson. Jefferson, however, clearly did not believe in the absolute separation dogma so dear to modern secularists.

As it happens, Thomas Jefferson was the first president of the Washington, D.C. school board[13] and was in fact the "chief author of the first plan of public education adopted for the city of Washington."[14] The first official report on file indicates that the Bible and the *Watts Hymnal* were the principal, if not the only, books then in use for reading by students.[15] If Jefferson were a strict separationist, he would never have tolerated such a practice. But strict separation-ism is a modern aberration. Government cooperation with religion—as long as government showed no sectarian bias—is what one finds in the historical record.

For example, the same Congress which drafted the Constitution also passed the Northwest Ordinance of 1787. That ordinance was the foundation of the American school system and stated that "religion, morality and knowledge" were necessary to good government and the happiness of mankind. The order of the three words cannot be accidental. Indeed, religion was part and parcel of the public school curriculum in the nineteenth century.

Textbooks from that time often referred to God, and did so without embarrassment. The public schools considered that one of their tasks was to develop character, and religion played a major role in that development. For example, the *New England Primer* opened with certain religious admonitions, followed by the Lord's Prayer, the Apostles' Creed, the Ten Commandments, and the names of the books of the Bible. The influence of William Holmes McGuffey of the University of Virginia was also far-reaching.

McGuffey's *Eclectic Readers* were published in 1836 and by 1920 had sold over 120 million copies, putting them in a class with only the Bible and *Webster's Dictionary*.[16] In short, the McGuffey books were the standard text. They also stressed "religion, morality, and knowledge," in that order.

Public schools in the United States once taught a Judeo-Christian ethic, which then constituted the dominant ethos. Though not perfect and often violated, it nevertheless provided American society with a cultural coherence and continuity that is now largely lost. Indeed the prevailing mood in the "public" schools is now one of hostility toward it and toward other forms of religious expression.

Should this be doubted, here are three examples of cases[17] from a wide collection that document separate and unequal treatment for religious citizens, along with disrespect for their civil rights.

Rebecca Higgins

On May 21, 1985, a student named Rebecca Higgins presented an oral book report to her sixth grade reading class at Venice Area Middle School near Tampa, Florida. The report was part of a class assignment in which students were encouraged to report on a subject of their choice and which appealed to their own personal interests. As it happened, Rebecca had a keen interest in the Bible and thus wrote her report on that subject. Her work included a 2″ × 2″ microfilm slide containing the Bible's entire contents. Rebecca's classmates received the report well, and the teacher gave her an "A."

After her discourse, and as part of her presentation, Rebecca offered copies of the New Testament only to those students who desired one. She further stated that anyone who took a copy and then subsequently wanted to return it was free to do so. Virtually all the students as well as the teacher took a copy.

However, about fifteen minutes into her next class, a teacher interrupted the proceedings and demanded that any students who had received Testaments hand them over to him. He provided no explanation as to why the students should hand over what was their property. Several students obeyed and turned over their copies, but some later confided to Rebecca that they kept theirs.

Later that day Rebecca went to a class held by this same teacher, who escorted her into the hall and told her that what she had done was "illegal," which implies criminal activity. It is noteworthy that the term "illegal" has come into play more in religious expression cases, rather than the charge of "unconstitutional," which even if untrue, as it usually is in these cases, would at least be more appropriate.

Later that day, Rebecca's reading teacher called her to a corner of the room. Still within hearing distance of her classmates, the teacher apologized to her for the turmoil over her report and the distribution of the New Testaments.

During other classes, and on the bus trip home, Rebecca attempted to return the Testaments to those whose copies had been in effect confiscated but who still desired to have them. She did the same the next day at school. At no time did her distribution of these Testaments interrupt or interfere with the normal school activities, and she conducted herself at all times in an orderly manner.

However, one visibly upset teacher demanded that the students return the books. This teacher took Rebecca aside, grilled her about her religious beliefs and affiliations, and told her not to distribute Bibles while on school property. This heavy-handed action led Rebecca's parents to file a lawsuit against the public school, charging that they had denied their daughter her rights. The parents prevailed,[18] but for the bulk of American history, such a case would have been unnecessary and unthinkable.

Students for Life

It is generally believed that free speech and free expression hold sway on American university campuses. While this is generally true, an incident at Oregon State University indicates that certain forms of speech and expression do not have an equal standing.

Posters on a variety of subjects usually adorn the student centers of colleges, as was the case at Oregon State. However, when Students for Life, a recognized student organization at Oregon State University, hung two posters showing detailed color photographs of babies who had been saline-poisoned and dismembered in abortions, the director of the student center ordered them removed. The reason? A handful of students had claimed to be "offended" by them.

In a subsequent meeting with the students, the director claimed that established policy required all posters to be "in good taste" and "not offensive to individuals or groups of individuals." Who was the judge of what was in good taste? The director told the students that he held absolute discretion in such matters.

In addition, the director warned the students that any attempt to replace the posters would result in lost privileges for Students for Life. Apparently, he was not only an authority on taste, but the sole dispenser of campus privileges as well. But the students weren't buying it. They believed that their constitutional rights had been violated and promptly filed suit.

In his deposition, the student center director relied on "community standards" to judge the posters, which he considered "offensive" and in violation of university policy. When asked to define community standards, he was forced to admit that the matter was completely subjective, citing the change in acceptance of publications such as *Playboy*, which was once considered objectionable.

The attorneys for the students argued that the policy was ambiguous and that the director's subjective interpretation had led to a "discriminatory impact" on the students' free speech rights. They also pointed out that while the pro-life posters had been removed, other posters on the National Socialist (Nazi) holocaust and Vietnam War had been left in place. Though these also showed scenes of carnage and death, the director had not considered them to be in bad taste.[19] Should the restriction stand, it would represent content-oriented censorship prohibited to school officials under the First Amendment. A federal court ruled in favor of the students,[20] but it is clearly the double standard of secularism that causes such cases.

Angela Guidry

Angela Guidry was the valedictorian of her public high school class in Moss Bluff, Louisiana. She prepared her valedictorian speech, and in May 1987 submitted a copy to the principal for review.

Guidry's text began by thanking "my Lord Jesus, who has allowed me to be in this position tonight." Following other introductory comments, Guidry added, "I'd like to share what's on my heart," and explained her personal source of motivation and fulfillment. She said: "To me the most important thing in your life is not whether you have a good education or a good job, but whether or not you have the Lord in your life." She went on: "It doesn't matter how many years you go to school or how successful you are in this life if you're not doing it all for the Lord."

After explaining her understanding of the need to acknowledge Jesus Christ as Savior, Angela then concluded: "My prayer and challenge for you tonight is that you would seek the Lord Jesus, believe in Him, and give your heart and life to Him."

As might be imagined, school officials were not pleased with the contents of the speech, and after a series of conflicts, the principal told Angela to delete all references to personal religious views. When Angela refused, the principal canceled her speech.

One could hardly think of a more flagrant denial of this student's constitutional rights, a denial based solely on the religious content of her speech. Clearly, the treatment she received was unequal and incredibly bigoted. A suit was subsequently filed in federal court.[21] But why should a suit be necessary? Only in a system dominated by the evangelists of secularism could a simple statement of religious belief, shared by countless people through the ages, cause such a stir.

I know of another instance in which a Christian teacher in a public school was told that if she mentioned God in the classroom she would be fired. Such cases, sadly, are far from rare.

State Interference

No one would deny that child abuse is a serious problem, but hysteria on the subject has given rise to reactionary responses that threaten the family. In particular, some social workers have become overzealous in their attempt to ferret out abusive parents.

For example, one disgruntled caller used a toll-free child-abuse hotline to charge that a Christian family in the neighborhood was sexually abusing their children. In short order, a squad of social workers and police invaded the home without regard for due process, took the children away from their parents, and placed them in a state institution. Medical examinations quickly revealed that no abuse of any sort had taken place.[22]

This type of action is sure to increase as laws give federal authorities more control over families. It also shows how such laws can be selectively applied against Christians.

Media Hostility

Few would deny that the media—especially the electronic media—constitute a force of unparalleled power and influence. It has been persuasively argued that television in itself is a negative influence because of the way it eschews moral judgments. Malcolm Muggeridge, a veteran television commentator, writes:

> [I]f it is the case, as I believe, that what we still call Western civilization is fast disintegrating, then the media are playing a major role in the process by carrying out, albeit for the most part unconsciously, a mighty brainwashing operation, whereby all traditional standards and values are being denigrated to the point of disappearing, leaving a moral vacuum in which the very concepts of Good and Evil have ceased to have any validity.[23]

The people who run mainstream media in the United States—especially the "electronic media"—are rigorously secular.[24] Given this rigidly secular profile, it is no surprise that they are often ignorant of religion in general and Christianity in particular. Quite frequently, they are hostile toward both. They have discerned that Christians are the last people who may be publicly defamed with impunity. The consequences of such defamation, when coupled with hostility from the state, are of the utmost seriousness.

Trends

In the Communist countries behind the Iron Curtain, religious believers have always been vilified by the official media and persecuted by the organs of the state. The persecutions have fluctuated according to the wishes of whatever dictator controlled the Party apparatus. Under the best conditions in Marxist-Leninist states, religion is entirely "privatized"—that is, allowed no public expression and permitted in controlled church settings only. As we saw with the eradication of religious symbols, there is much evidence that the tide of militant secularism is leading the United States in a similar direction.

The Reality Behind the Facade

Western movies give the illusion of bustling, thriving towns, but in reality the buildings are only one-dimensional fronts. Behind them is nothing but desert waste. Similarly, circus clowns paint smiles that mask their inner feelings.

America also has its fronts and grinning greasepaint: the Disneylands and Heritage USAs, the Magic Mountains and Universal Studios Tours. Americans sit for endless hours and laugh with Bill Cosby, Michael J. Fox, and other pied pipers from the fantasy world of television. But this genial facade hides an awful reality.

In contemporary America, unborn children are ripped from their mothers' wombs. Children with Down's syndrome are put on "low calorie" diets designed to starve them to death. Meanwhile, preachers tell people how to live happier lives. The American society that once held to a semblance of absolutes is gone. The last vestige of moral restraint has departed.

What does this all mean? One may safely say that

America is *already* under God's judgment. But this does not mean that one must give up.

The Need for a Response

Men have forgotten God; that's why all this happened. And as Edmund Burke noted, all that is necessary for evil to triumph is that good men do nothing.

Christian theism, especially since the Reformation, constituted a restraining influence against evil in all its forms, internal and external, which includes repressive government. And although the restraining influence of the Reformation was imperfect, as is everything and everyone in this world, there appears to be nothing fully capable of taking its place.

Hence, only a revitalized Christian church practicing true Christianity is capable of confronting the secular Goliath and the widespread havoc it has caused. Whether they feel "called" or not, Christians are the ones capable of providing any true direction to the culture.

PART TWO

A FALSE FAITH

Turning and turning in the widening gyre
The falcon cannot hear the falconer;
Things fall apart; the center cannot hold;
Mere anarchy is loosed upon the world,
The blood-dimmed tide is loosed, and everywhere
The ceremony of innocence is drowned;
The best lack all conviction, while the worst
Are full of passionate intensity.

—William Butler Yeats, *The Second Coming*

And Jesus entered the temple and cast out all those who
were buying and selling in the temple, and overturned the
tables of the money-changers and the seats of those who
were selling doves. And He said to them, "It is written, 'My
house shall be called a house of prayer;' but you are making
it a robbers' den."   —Matthew 21:12-13

Well, he went up to the preacher.
He went up to them all.
He told them all the same.
He said, "Sell all your jewelry and give it to the poor."
Well, they laid Jesus Christ in the grave.

—Woody Guthrie

One often hears the boast that there are fifty million evangelicals in the United States, but in light of the miniscule effect these alleged millions have had on contemporary culture, how could this possibly be true? Assuming for the moment that it is true, it should still be obvious that massive numbers of evangelicals are not enough in themselves to carry the day. It is also undeniable that the brand of Christianity practiced by American evangelicals, whatever their number, is not up to the task. This section will explore what may be called a false or at least an inadequate Christianity, along with false or inadequate methods that go along with it. We will return to some of these themes in the final section.

Accommodation

Surveying the pervasive secularism of our culture, it is harder still to deny that the Christian church has to a large degree made peace with it. In short, it has accommodated itself to a secular age, a serious matter since a dominant secularism, as Harvey Cox has pointed out, considers itself the sole belief system and never makes similar accommodations.

Accommodation also has a negative effect on the Christian psyche and on morale. Seeking approval from the world and attempting to accommodate secularism creates a second-class mentality among believers. Christians of this mentality are ineffective and will shirk their duty to stand for the truth. Whether they still believe the truth is another question.

The Question of Belief

A 1981 survey of 112 Protestant and Catholic theology professors found that 99 percent said they believed in God.

Moreover, 88 percent believed in eternal life and 83 percent in a final judgment. However, as one observer notes, it is quite probable that for a "significant number of these people, God, [eternal] life and final judgment were defined in a way that nineteenth-century Christians would have regarded as blasphemous."[1] Thus, as Michael Harrington writes:

> So when the same percentage confess belief in God in 1981 as did in 1881, that may conceal a transition from the God who spoke to Moses from the burning bush to Paul Tillich's "ground of being." Moreover, even though 83 percent of those respondents said they believed in final judgment, only 50 percent accepted the doctrine of hell . . . what is revealing is the way theologians privately and inconsistently decide which church truths they will accept. And it is of some moment that only 56 percent of the respondents had, over a decade, tried to convert someone.[2]

There is some irony in the fact that the one pointing out this crisis of belief among Christians is an atheist and a Socialist. The problem is doubtless more serious than he imagines. Many major Christian universities and seminaries have long since abandoned the concept that the Bible is true in all that it says.

It may well be that the huge numbers often bandied about may simply reflect those who identify with an American civil religion, which appears to be monotheistic and includes references to God in public ceremonies and on currency, but is far from being truly Christian. Pollster George Gallup has discovered that when he probed just how important religion is in the individual lives of various people, he found a pronounced "lack of substance behind the basic belief in God."[3] He adds:

[A]s a people, we lack deep levels of individual spiritual commitment. One sign of this is that the level of ethics in this country seems to be declining—at least in terms of public perceptions of ethical behavior. . . . We found there's very little difference between the churched and unchurched in terms of their general view on ethical matters and also their practical ethical responses in various situations.[4]

Another observer has pointed out that there is a tendency even among evangelical Christians to withhold the care of their souls from pastors and other believers and relegate it to psychotherapists.[5] This shift is hardly indicative of a robust faith. For their part, some pastors are too often prone to dispense cheap psychological bromides in their counseling, rather than the tough ethical standards of the New Testament. Too many Christian seminaries have sold their spiritual birthright for a bowl of psychological pottage.

Solzhenitsyn proclaims that "one word of truth outweighs the whole world,"[6] but Christians may well have forfeited their right to stand for the truth. With some notable exceptions, timidity is the rule. C. S. Lewis noted that Christians were often "tempted to make unnecessary concessions to those outside the Faith." They "gave in" too much, remained silent, and tended to "concede everything away."[7]

And when Christians are not accommodating themselves to the world, they are sometimes attempting to hide from it.

Phariseeism

The Gospels take note of the fact that the Jewish religious leaders of the day resented Jesus' practice of taking His

meals with tax collectors and "sinners."[8] It was the Pharisees' practice to maintain a policy of strict separation from
such hated and disreputable types. One spokesman for the
Pharisees indicated his motivation when he prayed: "God,
I thank You that I am not like other men—robbers, evil-
doers, adulterers—or even like this tax collector." He went
on to tell God what a wonderful fellow he was—in his
own eyes, of course—while the tax collector, in his prayer,
fully recognized his sin, and pleaded for mercy.[9]

While the Pharisees were a functioning part of society,
they had mastered the trick of so restricting their social
contacts that it amounted to a kind of monasticism. Indi-
vidually they were self-righteous, following a complicated
set of external rules, which were often easy to circumvent.
Collectively, their lives centered around what amounted to
a "holy club." The result was that they were harsh and
censorious to those outside their immediate circle. They
were a kind of Brahmin class who considered everyone else
lower-caste or even untouchables. Christ, however, willing-
ly embraced the outcasts, claiming that He had come to
save those who were lost.

In similar style, contemporary evangelicals often practice a legalistic form of righteousness. Legalism is the estab-
lishing of external rules or taboos by which Christians are
to live. These rules are usually extra-Biblical or rely on
certain Biblical verses conveniently removed from their
contexts. They posit a righteousness not based on what one
does, but on what one does *not* do: no dancing, smoking,
drinking, movies, music (other than "Christian"), card-
playing, etc. These rules and taboos serve as convenient
external checkpoints that indicate a supposed spirituality,
but which amounts only to a facade of righteousness, just as

it did for the Pharisees. Legalism makes it easy to judge others, but that judgment must inevitably be shallow, and not according to the heart. The legalist finds it easy to thank God that he is not like other people. There is a sense in which this preoccupation with one's spiritual facade might be called humanism, because this is not the righteousness that comes from God.

Modern Christians also emulate the Pharisees by retreating into a privatistic enclave, with similar results. This "club" atmosphere may explain the sharp racial divisions which are still to a great degree characteristic of American evangelicalism, even though the Scripture is clear that in the church "There is neither Jew nor Greek, slave nor free, male nor female, for you are all one in Christ Jesus."[10]

There is no record of Jesus requesting His followers to withdraw from the world, even though there was ample reason to do so, along with ample opportunity. In those days, there were a number of reclusive sects. Indeed, Jesus did not ask the Father to take His disciples out of the world, only that He "keep them from the evil one."[11] Withdrawal from the world is monasticism, and as British evangelical John R. W. Stott notes, monasticism "in whatever form is not a truly Christian ideal,"[12] precisely because it promotes such withdrawal. Stott has also noted that outsiders can easily sense when a church is a refuge *from* them rather than a ministry *for* them.

> To the outsider the church is often not inviting but forbidding, smugly satisfied with itself and harshly condemning of others. Non-Christians sometimes say that they find more acceptable, more compassionate understanding of human foibles in the world than in the church. To them the church is lacking in warmth, even positively inhuman.[13]

Evangelical monasticism may well be linked to problems of belief. It is entirely likely that many believers are unsure if their beliefs will stand up to what the world has to offer. Local churches often attempt to shield their flock from anything the leaders consider "harmful." This can only produce a nonthinking faith, capable only of retreat.

Sectarianism
Contemporary Christians not only retreat from the world, but also maintain themselves aloof from each other. While not accepting the grandiose institutional designs of the ecumenical movement, it is hard to deny that the church is overly divided, factionalized, and more characterized by infighting and jealousies than by a true spirit of love and cooperation. To the world, the Christian church seems a many-splintered thing, bound together by few, if any, underlying truths.

And to look at it from another angle, if Christians are continually fighting each other, their energies can hardly be taken up confronting the secular monolith. It may well be that sectarian strife results largely from a reluctance to undertake such confrontation. A soldier who attacks his comrade instead of the enemy is of little use on the battlefield; indeed, he is a positive hindrance. And it goes without saying that a house divided cannot stand.

Fatalism
Christian withdrawal can be due to prophetic fatalism, the idea that the world must soon end, hence any effort to "save" it is a waste of time and amounts to "polishing brass on a sinking ship," as it is sometimes put. The early apostles expected the consummation of the ages in their time,

but that did not cause them to congregate in holy clubs. Rather, they "went *into* all the world."

The fact of the matter is that the signs for the end have been present for ages. In addition, Jesus Christ Himself stated that only the Father knew the day and the hour.[14] One must be ready to depart anytime, but also ready for the long haul, being fully aware in both cases that God is in control.

Evangelism and Social Concern

A monastic attitude is also due to confusion about the relationship between evangelism and "social concern." In its most extreme formulation, the thesis of this mindset is that God's only concern is the salvation of individual souls, and that anything else is a heretical, watered-down "social gospel" that must be rejected by the faithful. While this view claims Biblical fidelity, that is far from the case, as John Stott explains:

> This kind of evangelicalism which concentrates exclusively on saving individual souls is not true evangelicalism. It is not evangelical because it is not biblical. It forgets that God did not create souls but body-souls called human beings, who are also social beings, and that He cares about their bodies and their society as well as about their relationship with Himself and their eternal destiny. So true Christian love will care for people as people, and will seek to serve them, neglecting neither the soul for the body nor the body for the soul. As a matter of fact, it has not been characteristic of evangelicals in the past to be shy of social action, or even, when necessary, of political action.[15]

The involvement of Christians in the fight against slavery is only one example of past "social action" by Christians. Slave owners of the time considered such activism to be religious meddling and a humanistic "social gospel." George Mueller's work with orphans is another of many examples.

Whatever the reasons for it, and whatever one chooses to call it, contemporary Christian monasticism is an inadequate response to the challenges of this age. In addition, just as it is impossible to "stay out of politics," it is impossible to withdraw completely from the world. Phariseeism is thus not only wrong, but guaranteed to fail.

Christian Utopia?

While some Christians are busy avoiding the world around them, others go to the opposite extreme. They believe Christians are destined to take over and rule the world, not by violent revolution, but by gradually "taking dominion" of the political process until the "righteous," *viz*, themselves, hold the reigns of power and reinstitute Old Testament law. As those who would rule like to put it, it is not they who are actually in charge, but God, albeit ruling through His chosen intermediaries.

This is, in short, a theocratic position. At best, it is a minority movement, though, like the Christian Left of *Sojourners* and *The Other Side*, its influence is often out of proportion to its numbers.

In the past such views have been associated with postmillennialism, the idea that the *church*, not the return of Jesus Christ, will bring in the kingdom of God on earth. But what might be called the "takeover" perspective really, in many instances, has more to do with utopianism than Biblical exegesis.

Psychologists such as Erik Erikson have pointed out

that humans have a strong, inbred tendency toward utopianism, a "universal nostalgia for a lost paradise."[16] Thus, utopianism comes "naturally," and might even be considered humanistic. Moreover, history is littered with the wreckage of failed utopian experiments, many undertaken by Christians, some well-meaning, others not. This latest takeover experiment would fail as well, for obvious reasons.

In the first place, Scripture is clear that there are none righteous, and that Christians are but repentant sinners. The dominion impulse spoken of in the first chapter of Genesis, when tainted by sin and the Fall, and not restrained by Christian justice, has produced campaigns of terror.

Second, Christian faith and spirituality are no guarantee of political competence, wise governance, or fairness in dealing with the public. To believe that they are is naive and dangerous, and contrary to all observation.

Third, the historical record shows that power corrupts, and that even Christians can be, and are, corrupted by power.

Those who drafted the United States Constitution were all too aware of the sinfulness of man and the possibility of corruption, even among the openly religious. They disbelieved in the divine right of kings and knew what mischief could be caused by absolute monarchs who arrogated to themselves the title "defender of the faith." More important, they also knew full well that no sinful human being was to be trusted with absolute power, and hence set up an elaborate system of checks and balances for purposes of restraint. James Madison and other Framers recognized that if men were angels there would be no need for government. But men are not angels, so they designed a system for sinners.

In addition, Christians currently have their hands full operating their various churches and organizations, which are not always models of either efficiency or righteousness. One also observes that Christians even of the same theological and political beliefs, and who operate in the same organization are often at each other's throats. How can those unable to successfully run a small organization and get along with their own families expect to rule a modern state, especially a state in which vast numbers of people disagree with those who see themselves as chosen to rule?

Christians have every right to be involved in the political process, but they must rid themselves of the notion that they are going to assume control of other people and governments and rule the world. Many of those who believe they can do this are guilty of hubris.

The believer's claim must not be for absolute power, but for equality in the marketplace of ideas, where Christianity, and the worldview that springs from it, can more than hold their own. It is hard to imagine how claims of special righteousness and a divine right to rule will help Christians gain this equal hearing. Indeed, it may well create a backlash.

The Political Gospel

As noted, Christians have the right to be involved in the political process and must do so if they are to fulfill their responsibilities of stewardship and care toward their fellows. Their full-throated assertion of this right in recent times has caused much distress to the secular establishment, which has tended to view religious people in general and Christians in particular as second-class citizens or even enemies, and which tries to exclude them from the public realm whenever possible.

But there has also been a tendency to put too much faith in the political process, which at times can be as corrupt as the Mafia. While there are certainly many grievances which can and should be addressed through political channels, Christians above all people should realize that what can be accomplished through institutions is necessarily limited, and that matters of the heart and spirit are of primary importance. Legislative influence, direct-mail fund-raising, political action committees, press releases, lobbying campaigns, and other sundry activisms may be effective and appropriate in their place, but they are not the sum total of the Christian faith.

The church has lost sight of the truth that we struggle not against "flesh and blood" but against spiritual forces.[17] In like manner, "the weapons of our warfare are not of the flesh, but divinely powerful for the destruction of fortresses."[18] Trusting in politics as a cure-all is an illusion. The ballot box is indeed a valued and necessary feature of democracy, but to see the ballot box as the answer to all mankind's ills is a purely humanistic prescription.

Hyperactivity

Those who overly indulge the political realm or throw themselves into frenzied activity in any other area, including church activities, risk burning themselves out and jeopardizing their families.

As meaningful contact between parents and their children has decreased, parents and children have steadily become strangers, even in their own homes. This can cause a breakdown in human development, because it is the family that builds healthy people—physically, mentally, and spiritually.

Parents must keep themselves within the family environment. Fathers and mothers who are workaholics are not good parents, even if they are off saving America from "secular humanism." Children are more important than the cars, houses, and other toys that occupy many modern parents.

Show Business Christianity

Not so long ago, modern Christians discovered television, and many have since come to regard the medium as something of a savior. Through the miracle of technology, it was thought, one man in a studio could reach the masses.

However, there are several reasons why television is an unsuitable medium for the presentation of the gospel. Indeed, it is highly questionable whether any authentic religious experience can be communicated through television.

First, there is a sense in which the medium is the message, to use McLuhan's famous aphorism. Television is something you *watch* and hence favors moods of passivity and conciliation. It is at its best when serious content of any kind is muted and is above all a notoriously "dumb" medium best suited to entertainment. As professor Neil Postman, author of *Amusing Ourselves to Death,* notes, television strips away everything that makes religion an historic, profound, and sacred activity. On television, "there is no ritual, no dogma, no tradition, no theology, and above all, no sense of spiritual transcendence." A television preacher may talk about God, but God is invisible, an off-stage character, and the viewers see only the preacher. "On these shows," Postman adds, "the preacher is tops. God comes out as second banana."[19]

It might be noted at this point that television is not really "communication," which implies reciprocity. The audience can see the preacher, but the preacher cannot see them. The communication, such as it is, is all one way. The instrument is a propagandist's dream. One may well imagine what Hitler and Stalin would have done with it.

Second, there is no way to consecrate the space in which a television show is experienced. This is not to say that religious experience must take place only in special buildings or places. But for it to take place anywhere, there is usually some change of symbol—candles, a cross, etc.— some alteration of decor indicating a transfer from profane to sacred use. Behavior changes as well.

While watching common television fare such as "Cheers" or "The Cosby Show," people eat, talk, or even do pushups. The figures on the screen do not mind; they have no way of finding out what is going on. There is frequently no change from that distracted state of mind when the show is overtly religious.[20] And one negative implication of television Christianity is that, since you can watch it all right at home, there is little or no need for the local church.

Third, television has a strong and inherent bias toward a psychology of secularism. Neil Postman's observations are worth quoting at length:

> The screen is so saturated with our memories of profane events, so deeply associated with the commercial and entertainment worlds that it is difficult for it to be recreated as a

frame for sacred events. Among other things, the viewer is aware that a flick of the switch will produce a different and secular event on the screen—a hockey game, a commercial, a cartoon. . . . Both the history and the ever-present possibilities of the television screen work against the idea that introspection or spiritual transcendence is desirable in its presence. The television screen wants you to remember that its imagery is always available for your amusement and pleasure.[21]

Fourth, as Malcolm Muggeridge observes, the effect of television is to "draw people away from reality" and into fantasy.[22] The camera "always lies,"[23] says Muggeridge, who relates a fascinating "Fourth Temptation" in which the Devil offers Jesus free television time. Far from seizing the opportunity to relay His message far and wide, the Savior refuses the offer.[24]

Television is indeed an awesome force, but the inherently fanciful and mendacious nature of the medium clearly makes the communication of truth a difficult if not impossible matter.

The Entertainment Gospel

It seems evident that television Christianity, far from changing the situation for the better, has in fact adapted itself to the medium and become entertainment. Many shows put a premium on music. Instead of solid teaching, there is a talk-show format hosted by the "star," the high-profile "television personality," and sometimes his wife, along with celebrity guests. These, not God, are the stars of the show, even though they might not wish it to be so. Neil Postman cites the constant danger of idolatry, and even of "blasphemy"[25] in such circumstances.

Television Christianity loves the loud, the sensational, the flashy. There are the theatrics of faith healers restoring the hangnail of a viewer a thousand miles away, or a woman selling crosses that glow in the dark, or a screaming, sputtering evangelist mispronouncing words he does not understand. All one need do is view two hours of this tawdry and dismal fare to see how bad things really are. Woody Allen was doubtless right when, in his film *Hannah and Her Sisters,* he wondered whether Jesus' reaction on seeing what was done in His name might be to vomit.

But, unfortunately, the entertainment dimension is far from the only pitfall of television Christianity.

The Gospel of Wealth

Producing a television show of any size is an expensive proposition. Those who would survive in this highly competitive world must therefore attract the largest audience possible, and this applies to religious broadcasters as well. The executive director of the National Religious Broadcasters Association sums up the unwritten law of all television preachers: "[Y]ou can get your share of the audience only by offering people something they want."[26]

This is a rather unusual credo for religious leaders, who instead of offering people what they want normally tell them what they need, or what they must sacrifice. Jesus Christ told people to count the cost before following Him, and clearly indicated that in this world, Christians would experience many troubles.

Neil Postman notes that religious programs, like their secular counterparts, are filled with good cheer (what media gurus call "happy talk") and that they "celebrate affluence." He further speculates that it is precisely *because* the message is trivial that the shows have high ratings.[27] It is either openly proclaimed or subtly implied that by supporting the television ministry, you too can be wealthy, just like the hosts.

The grim truth is that, on television, the big-name star and his prosperity gospel come across better than God and truth. True Christianity is difficult, serious, and on many points offensive to modern thinking. What might be called the "Lite" television version is too often easy and amusing, and one can argue that it is a different kind of religion altogether. Defenders of televangelism argue that some people do in fact get converted or gain spiritual help from it. But even assuming this is so, it still does not validate the medium of television as a gospel tool any more than it would validate the Elmer Gantrys of the world who distort the truth with fantasy.

The entertainment and prosperity gospels not only fail to do the job, but they hurt the witness of the church as well. One legacy of television Christianity is that far too many local churches are built around a celebrity pastor or music director, and now seem to be more oriented to entertainment than to teaching and worship. This is tragic.

Recent sexual and financial scandals may awaken Christians to the great abuses that presently occur and, hopefully, lead to a wider debate about the validity of television Christianity altogether. But whether it lingers on, as seems likely, or begins to fade away, televised religion fails to meet the challenge of secular culture. When it is not self-satirizing, which is often, it provides endless fodder for cartoonists and comedians.

Intellectual Illiteracy

In terms of their intellectual content, the purveyors of television Christianity certainly do not measure up to many pastors, elders, seminary professors, or even laymen. However, it is also true that many of the leading lights of the evangelical world, as Neil Postman also notes,

> do not compare favorably with well-known evangelicals of an earlier period, such as Jonathan Edwards, George Whitefield and Charles Finney, who were men of great learning, theological subtlety and powerful expositional skills.[28]

These men, and others like them, influenced the whole climate of religious life in Europe and in North America. For example, John Nelson Darby and William Kelly developed the theology of dispensationalism and are considered by some to be the originators of what is now called fundamentalism. Yet both were men of enormous erudition, among the most learned of their time. Professor Postman also states:

> In the eighteenth and nineteenth centuries, religious thought and institutions in America were dominated by an austere, learned, and intellectual form of discourse that is largely absent from religious life today.[29]

What the early church, the Reformers, and those mentioned above knew full well was that Christianity speaks to *all* of life: science, philosophy, art, politics, medicine, and so on. Their view of life was comprehensive in regard to the truth. For them, *all* truth was God's truth.

For the most part, it has been downhill since that time,

to the point that much of contemporary Christianity can safely be characterized as anti-intellectual. The comprehensive view of life and truth has all but disappeared and has been replaced by a highly compartmentalized and fragmented view that keeps certain disciplines and areas of inquiry off-limits.

The fault does not lie entirely with the church. Modern culture, especially since the 1960s, is also highly anti-intellectual, sentimental, and of course secularized. The church, however, has not provided a bulwark against these trends, as British writer Harry Blamires recognizes:

> But unfortunately the Christian mind has succumbed to the secular drift with a degree of weakness and nervelessness unmatched in Christian history. It is difficult to do justice in words to the complete loss of intellectual morale in the twentieth-century Church. One cannot characterize it without having recourse to language which will sound hysterical and melodramatic.[30]

One sometimes hears it said of a preacher or scholar that he or she has "head knowledge" rather than "heart knowledge." The implication is that such ones are stuffed with theological facts, but are essentially cold and unfeeling inside. That may be true in some cases. God knows the hearts. But what it more likely indicates is that the listener's shallow brand of Christianity had simply rendered him incapable of understanding what was being said. And instead of taking stock of his own deficiencies, he took the easy way out and imputed the problem to the speaker. It is a form of blaming the messenger if one does not like the message.

Another clue to the current climate of anti-intellectualism is that preachers are encouraged to "dumb down" their sermons, rather than present something intellectually challenging. Such sermons often aim at everyone in general and hence speak to no one in particular.

Above all, it is heard, one must "preach a simple gospel," but this common formulation is misleading. One may preach the gospel simply, but no Christian, if he is faithful to the Scriptures, preaches a "simple" gospel. The gospel is the eternal God's revelation of Himself in human form and in human history. It is an absolutely stupendous historical event which touches virtually all areas of life and creates countless questions, most of them quite complicated. And as Francis Schaeffer noted, an honest question requires an honest answer. As much as possible, the Christian should be capable of providing that answer. Spiritual slogans will not do the job.

This is not an apology for a dry intellectualism, a highbrow or snobbish posture, nor for a view that sees the gospel only in terms of ideas. Neither is it a denial of the role of the Holy Spirit in conversion and the Christian life. Rather it is simply a recognition that a gospel which fails to grapple with all of life is a false gospel, certain to fail in view of the present opposition and light-years away from what was once characteristic of the Christian church. In the simplest possible terms, the contemporary church has lost its mind.

Cultural Illiteracy

The traditional view of the church has been that the arts, human creativity, and the beauty of the world are gifts of God and thus need no justification on spiritual or utilitarian grounds. They are what they are and were put here for people's enjoyment. However, modern Christianity has largely lost this truth. One would be hard-pressed to find many leading artists who are true believers. Indeed, the situation is depressing to say the least.

Almost everywhere one looks in modern Christianity there is a lack of craftsmanship—in publishing, in music, and particularly in the hucksterism of television. Some prime samples of Christian endeavor in the arts may be found in the local Christian bookstore, which, often as not, is not primarily a bookstore at all, but rather a kind of accessory and paraphernalia shop. One author's pointed remarks are worth quoting at length:

> For the coffee table we have a set of praying hands made out of some sort of pressed muck. Christian posters are ready to adorn your walls with suitable Christian graffiti to sanctify them and make them a justifiable expense. Perhaps a little plastic cube with a mustard seed entombed within to boost your understanding of faith. . . . On a flimsy rack are stacked a pile of records. You may choose them at random blind-folded, for most of them will be the same idle rehash of acceptable spiritual slogans, endlessly recycled as pablum for the tone-deaf, television-softened brains of your present-day Christians. . . . The airwaves as you leave the shop are jammed with a choice avalanche of what can generally be summed up as rubbish, ready to clog your television and radio set with "Christian" programming. The publishing houses churn out (measured by the ton) a landslide of material which can scarcely be called books, often composed of the same themes which are viewed as spiritual, rehashed endlessly by writers who would be better employed in another trade.[31]

To be sure, the standards of the world are also about as low as they can be, but this does not mean that Christians should adopt mediocrity as their standard.

Art provides the antennae of a culture, and it seems clear that too many Christians have ceased to pay attention. In the artistic realm, as in the spiritual, many have lost themselves in a religious ghetto where the constant cross-pollination of ideas is by and large only with other Christians. They thus miss an important point of contact with precisely those non-Christians with whom they have at least some common interest.

Artistically, the result is usually pablum, and the "circle think" mentality hinders quality work and presents a form of unreality as to how believers should conduct themselves in the world around them. A root problem is the mistaken idea that anything outside so-called "spiritual" endeavors is evil. As noted, this is neither the view of the Bible nor the Christian church through the centuries.

The great majority of Christians have no view of the arts because they do not view the arts. They have no view of cinema because they do not go to movies. They have no view of ballet or the theater because they do not attend ballet or the theater. They have no view of music because they either refuse or are afraid to listen to anything other than "Christian" music.

It should be stressed that being "tuned in" to the arts is an exercise in understanding the culture around us. It is not the same as accommodation—that is, adopting the beliefs and views of the dominant culture. To cut oneself off from this vital area of life is to be a cultural illiterate. Little wonder that Christians are often perceived as kooks, obscurantists or cultural neanderthals. In too many cases, this perception is true.

A Church Under Judgment
In the first part of this book we noted the present condition of the world and that it is under God's judgment. Few, if any, understanding Christians would disagree with that assessment. However, this judgment is not cause for self-congratulation, especially in view of what we have just outlined.

Scripture is equally clear that judgment begins not with the world and those who oppose God but, rather, with "us," the family of God, the church.[32] Given the terrible condition of the world, the woefully inadequate response of the church, and the sure hand of God's judgment, it would seem clear that the only acceptable solution is a return to true Christianity. To that we now turn.

PART THREE

TRUE CHRISTIANITY

Surely some revelation is at hand;
Surely the Second Coming is at hand.
The Second Coming! Hardly are those words out
When a vast image out of *Spiritus Mundi*
Troubles my sight; somewhere in sands of the desert
A shape with lion body and the head of a man,
A gaze blank and pitiless as the sun,
Is moving its slow thighs, while all about it
Reel shadows of the indignant desert birds.
The Darkness drops again; but now I know
That twenty centuries of stony sleep
Were vexed to nightmare by a rocking cradle,
And what rough beast, its hour come round at last,
Slouches towards Bethlehem to be born?
       — William Butler Yeats, *The Second Coming*

*A*s we stated at the outset, the destructive legacy of militant secularism is evident on every hand, with the result that many, especially on the Left, are in despair. For example, Christopher Lasch writes:

57

The Nazi holocaust, the threat of nuclear annihilation, the depletion of natural resources, well-founded predictions of ecological disaster have fulfilled the poetic prophecy, giving concrete historical substance to the nightmare, or death wish, that avant-garde artists were first to express. The question of whether the world will end in fire or in ice, with a bang or a whimper, no longer interests artists alone. Impending disaster has become an everyday concern, so commonplace and familiar that nobody any longer gives much thought to how disaster might be averted.[1]

The Christian, however, need not share this bleak outlook, even though the present situation presents the church with perhaps its stiffest challenge in modern times.

Current struggles in the world are not only over beliefs and ideas but also involve institutions. More important—and this is of special concern to believers—the very lives and souls of human beings are in play. We have now noted what kind of Christian faith and experience fails to meet the challenge. What then must be done?

Curiously, it is sometimes the non-Christian who sees the need for precisely what true Christianity can offer. For example, French existentialist Albert Camus claimed to believe in nothing, and to consider everything absurd. But he was also an honest thinker, and perhaps because of this honesty, along with his absence of belief, was able to see the needs of the age in a way matched by few of his peers. He wrote:

The world expects of Christians that they will raise their voices so loudly and clearly and so formulate their protest that not even the simplest man can have the slightest doubt about what they are saying. Further, the world expects of Christians that they will eschew all fuzzy abstractions and plant themselves squarely in front of the bloody face of history. We stand in need of folk who have determined to speak directly and unmistakably and come what may, to stand by what they have said.[2]

Notice that there is no doubt in Camus' mind that Christianity is inherently *opposed* to the spirit of the age, what he calls the "bloody face of history." By this standard, an accommodationist posture is fatal. Camus expects Christians to spurn abstractions and hold clear, well-defined beliefs. They must not only raise their voices, but do so loudly, and in such a way as there is no doubt as to what is being said. That done, Camus says, they must stand by what they have said. One could hardly put it any better. The believer who would practice true Christianity will share the spirit of Isaiah the prophet and say, "Here I am. Send me!"[3]

Not only so, but there should be a fervor behind this sentiment. Christians should at times be Rachel weeping, but there is also a place for them to be angry and outraged. Believers and nonbelievers alike should be jumping to their feet screaming for it all to stop.

It is now time to turn our attention to the genuine article, a true Christianity capable of meeting this challenge. This brand of Christianity will, of necessity, concern itself with questions of faith and institutions. We shall begin with questions of belief.

The True God
The essence of true Christianity is the drive for communion (and eventually union) with God, both internally and externally. True Christianity has to do with the life of the

Spirit. It is the internalization of truth, but also the externalization of that same truth as the person matures spiritually. As this takes place, the believer is able to reflect in substance the character of the Creator.

The Creator, it should be understood, is the eternal and omnipotent God of Scripture, not some limited abstraction or wistful projection of human attributes. He is the omnipotent, all-knowing God who created all things *ex nihilo*, from the vast galaxies in space to the tiniest grain of sand.

This omnipotent God exists in real space-time history; as Francis Schaeffer put it, He is the God who is "there." Nothing is beyond His power. Hence, the Christian takes the miraculous for granted and sees God's presence and imprint in all areas of life. After I had become a believer, this was something that struck me as fundamental to all existence.

Christians hold that God has revealed Himself, specifically His character, through various laws and principles expressed in the Bible: the Ten Commandments, the Sermon on the Mount, and the teachings of the apostles found in the letters of the New Testament. The God revealed in the Bible is both a holy God and a righteous God.

The Cure for the Fall

As noted, true Christianity explains the present abnormality of people and the world around us in terms of the flaws caused by the historic, space-time Fall. This Fall tainted all facets of the human being and blighted nature as well. Moreover, the effects of the Fall are all-pervasive and have been passed on to every member of the human race, all of whom are sinners.

Modern thinkers are fond of deriding the Scriptures and like to believe that man is basically good. But they have no real answer to the fact that people's supposedly noble attributes are vitiated by selfishness, cruelty, and vice. They also like to think of God as pure benevolence, or some sort of New Age "Life Force," but this is not the picture that emerges in the Old and New Testaments, as one writer explains:

> The tension between God's holy righteousness and his compassionate mercy cannot be legitimately resolved by remolding his character into an image of pure benevolence as the church did in the nineteenth century. There is only one way that this contradiction can be removed; through the cross of Christ which reveals the severity of God's anger against sin and the depth of his compassion in paying its penalty through the vicarious sacrifice of his Son. In systems which resolve this tension by softening the character of God, Christ and his work become an addendum, and spiritual darkness becomes complete because the true God has been abandoned for the worship of a magnified image of human tolerance.[4]

As noted above, true Christianity provides the answer to the Fall in the atoning work of Jesus Christ on the cross. And through His resurrection, a central doctrine of true Christianity, Christ proved to be the only begotten Son of God. He was "declared with power to be the Son of God by the resurrection from the dead."[5] In addition:

> "God has fulfilled this promise to our children in that He raised up Jesus, as it is also written in the second Psalm, 'Thou art My Son; today I have begotten Thee.' "[6]

As the Apostle Paul perceptively wrote, "if Christ has not been raised, then our preaching is in vain, your faith also is vain."[7] But Christ has been raised from the dead, and the empty tomb means that no mere man died at Calvary. Christ now reigns as Lord over a new spiritual community of believers. He is the second Adam, a "life-giving spirit."[8] Where the first Adam was an "earthly" being, "the second man is from heaven."[9] Jesus Christ is the new King of creation, "the faithful witness, the first-born of the dead, and the ruler of the kings of the earth."[10]

God grants full forgiveness of sin to those who by faith accept Christ's redemptive work. This does not mean that those who believe are thereby perfect. To put it in medical terms, the fatal infection of sin is cured through Christ's work on the cross, but the symptoms and effects remain. The believer is substantially healed by Christ's work, but he or she is never perfect in this life. But through Christ's voluntary death for our sins, God's justice and love are reconciled, and the way of salvation opened for those who accept the gift of God by faith in Jesus Christ.

In the words of the Westminster Catechism, the chief end of man is to glorify God and enjoy Him forever. Such a statement often seems absurd to non-Christians, but Malcolm Muggeridge, who was converted later in life, noted that one of the greatest attractions of Christianity is "its sheer absurdity." He writes:

> I love all those crazy sayings in the New Testament—which, incidentally, turn out to be literally true—about how fools and illiterates and children understand what Jesus was talking about better than the wise, the learned and the venerable; about how the poor, not the rich, are blessed, the meek, not

the arrogant, inherit the earth, and the pure in heart, not the strong in mind, see God.[11]

True Human Beings

True Christianity posits the belief that people are created in the image of God. This means that both Christians and non-Christians, like God, have personhood, a measure of self-transcendence, intelligence, morality, love, and creativity. They are not one-dimensional biological machines but three-dimensional human beings possessing great dignity and worth. Such dignity and worth also imply responsibility and accountability. To deny or avoid responsibility for one's actions is not only to flout God, it is to act in a way that is less than human.

Spiritual Power

The believer needs the absolutes of the Bible to transform, order, and direct the fallen nature. This is necessary because the believer is always in a spiritual state of *becoming*—never attaining the complete spiritual fulfillment because in this life, again, there is only substantial healing of the fallen nature. As the Apostle Paul notes, "now we see in a mirror dimly, but then face to face; now I know in part, but then I shall know fully just as I also have been fully known."[12]

Fortunately, however, God has not left believers without provision to grow spiritually, to become what they are capable of becoming in Jesus Christ. They share in Christ's resurrected power and are part of a new spiritual community. (This will be discussed in the section on the church.) This power is most necessary, since all true Christians will be resisted by opposing forces in the spiritual realm. The Apostle Paul writes:

Our struggle is not against flesh and blood, but against the rulers, against the spiritual forces of wickedness in the heavenly places.[13]

If the believer is practicing consistent Scriptural living, he or she will inevitably struggle against demonic powers. In the final analysis that is the nature of true Christianity. Christians who are not being opposed need to examine the way they are living their lives.

Awesome Freedom

Christ is the truth incarnate, and He told His followers that "the truth shall make you free."[14] Believers are free from the guilt of sin by way of the atonement and continuing repentance. They are free from the rigors of Old Testament laws and ceremonies, and are also free from the petty legalisms modern Christians often inflict on those around them. Christians are, in short, free to be and become what God intended when He first created man.

Such *awesome freedom* is only possible through Jesus Christ. The believer is, in effect, "crucified with Christ," so that even though he continues in the natural world, "it is no longer I who live, but Christ lives in me." The life that we now live "in the flesh" we live "by faith in the Son of God, who loved me, and delivered Himself up for me."[15] Allowing Christ to live through the believer brings forth the fruit of the Holy Spirit: "love, joy, peace, patience, kindness, goodness, faithfulness, gentleness, self-control."[16]

Russian writer Fyodor Dostoyevsky describes this freedom in his novel *The Brothers Karamazov*, in the context of the temptation of Christ. Satan first tempted Christ by saying, "If you are the Son of God, command that these stones become bread."[17] Of course, being the very God that He is, He could easily have turned the stones into bread, and the people would have followed and worshiped Him for it.

Dostoyevsky notes that one reason Christ declined to perform the miracle was because He did not want to deprive people of their freedom, for obedience bought with a price is not the spiritual freedom that Christ desired for His followers.[18] One should add that Christ also refused because the request came from Satan, and because, as He stated in His reply, it was written that "man shall not live on bread alone, but on every word that proceeds out of the mouth of God."[19]

The Word of God provides the substance of which true freedom is composed. It is, so to speak, the freedom of not having to look over one's shoulder, the freedom to forget one's past, a freedom from guilt. It is a freedom to enjoy the Creator, a freedom to do those things pleasing to God. The Apostle Paul noted that believers were called to freedom, but cautioned them not to "turn your freedom into an opportunity for the flesh."[20] Instead, they were to serve one another in love, which is in keeping with the commandment to love one's neighbor as oneself. One of the fruits of the Spirit is joy, and I want to emphasize that the believer has the freedom to enjoy life. The rigid rules enforced by some churches constitute a form of bondage, and bondage is not true Christianity. God did not place His creatures in a concentration camp, but in a paradise. Moreover, Jesus Christ was a person who obviously enjoyed Himself. Indeed, this was one of the complaints against

Him on the part of the self-righteous Pharisees, evidently a sullen, dour lot. They called Christ a "gluttonous man and a drunkard, a friend of tax-gatherers and sinners."[21]

In summary, freedom in its essence means to enjoy God and His creation and to enjoy life. It means to do good in service to both God and human beings. It is found only in Jesus Christ.

The Church

God has not left believers in Jesus Christ on their own. Indeed, wherever two or three Christians gather in His name, Christ promises that "there I am in their midst."[22]

All Christians are part of the *ecclesia*, a Greek term meaning "called-out company" from which our word church derives. When Christ ascended into Heaven, the believers still on earth effectively became His body, energized by the Holy Spirit whom He sent to complete His work. Christ is the Head of that body.[23] When anyone is converted, the Holy Spirit baptizes them into the body of Christ, the universal church. This universal church includes all believers of all times and places. The *visible* church is the worldwide body of believers, in all its diversity, in its institutional form.

The *local* church, it should be stressed, is not the building. In fact, the early concept of the local church had *no* connection with a building. For example, Paul sends his greetings to a group of believers by stating, "greet the church that is in their house."[24] Paul's reference to the church is not to a building but to the "church" (believers) "in" the house.

The local church, then, is a congregation or gathering of Christians in a specific place. It is a living entity and meets in a building. And, as we saw, in New Testament times believers often met in houses. In the Communist bloc, believers meet wherever and whenever they can. But however it is they meet, the Scriptures set forth certain norms.

First, it is a given that churches should be composed of believers in Jesus Christ. Second, these congregations should meet together in a special way on the first day of the week.[25] Third, there are to be elders who have responsibility for oversight of the church. Fourth, there are to be pastors and teachers who feed and care for the flock. Fifth, there are to be deacons, responsible for the material side of church affairs.[26] There are clearly defined standards for those who would hold all these offices.[27] The church, it should be stressed, has no authority to change or diminish these standards, nor to elevate any other standards above them.

Sixth, the local church is to take seriously the discipline of the believers within that congregation. Seventh, there is a place for organization on a wider basis than the local church, such as councils and conferences.[28] Eighth, the two sacraments of baptism and the Lord's supper are to be practiced.[29]

Some would question whether some of these are actually norms, or whether others are in fact commanded. It should be stressed that the primary point is that there is a place for the local church and that the Scriptures do contain guidelines for it. At the same time, however, there are vast areas of freedom for change. No one has the right to bind men morally where the Scripture lacks a clear command.

However, the local church must face reality. It must

divest itself of the "entertainment" mentality and again become a center of worship, instruction, and true fellowship. It should restore the power-packed hymns of the past and eschew trivial songs which basically tell how the singer feels about Jesus, but little about the Savior Himself. In this age of show business, there is ample entertainment in the dominant culture. Imagine a college professor breaking into song in the middle of a lecture. It is just as ludicrous to turn a worship service into a show. The church should not be in the business of duplicating current trends.

The local church is not to be bound in a straightjacket. There is freedom in Christ. Anything the New Testament does not command concerning church form is a freedom to be exercised under the leadership of the Holy Spirit for that particular time and place. In other words, the New Testament sets boundaries, but within these boundaries there is much freedom of movement to meet the changes that may arise in different places and times.[30]

Confrontation

The church provides Christians with a place of fellowship, spiritual sustenance, and worship. But the church is also the "pillar and foundation of the truth,"[31] and the present age has no desire to hear the truth, which it finds offensive. True Christianity is likewise offensive to the secular juggernaut. It is light to their darkness. A confrontation is therefore inevitable if the church is faithful to its mandate.

However, it is often in moments of great confrontation and controversy that the truth is most effectively spoken. For example, the Apostle Paul took advantage of every confrontational situation to speak about Christ. Paul had been arrested and beaten in Jerusalem for his stand for the truth. He so inflamed the people that he had to be guarded by Roman soldiers. As these led him away, he begged to be allowed to speak to the people[32] and from there proclaimed the gospel of Christ.

Controversial and Dogmatic

Modern Christianity likes to represent Jesus Christ as a meek, harmless friend of the world, but that is not the picture found in the Gospels nor the book of Revelation. Far from being passive and meek, Christ was both avidly controversial and dogmatic.

Indeed, as John R. W. Stott explains, Christianity is inevitably and "essentially dogmatic"

> because it purports to be a revealed faith. If the Christian religion were just a collection of the philosophical and ethical ideas of men (like Hinduism), dogmatism would be entirely out of place. But if God has spoken (as Christians claim), both in olden days through the prophets and in these last days through His Son, why should it be thought "dogmatic" to believe His Word ourselves and to urge other people to believe it too?[33]

Stott adds that Jesus Christ was not "broadminded" in the popular sense of that word. That is, He was not prepared to accept as valid any views on any subject. He was unafraid to dissent from official doctrines He knew to be wrong and to expose error. He called false teachers "blind guides," "wolves in sheep's clothing," "whitewashed tombs," and even "a brood of vipers."

Christ was literally on the offensive, with a message that often offended those around Him, to the point that they wanted to kill Him. One might say that he took "affirmative action" against evil. One illustration is the incident in which Jesus

> cast out all those who were buying and selling in the temple, and overturned the tables of the money-changers and the seats of those who were selling doves. And He said to them, "It is written, 'My house shall be called a house of prayer'; but you are making it a robbers' den."[34]

In addition, Jesus would not permit anyone to carry goods through the Temple and even blocked the doorways.[35]

In short, Jesus took the truth to the world, and commanded His disciples to do likewise:

> And Jesus came up and spoke to them, saying, "All authority has been given to Me in heaven and on earth. Go therefore and make disciples of all the nations, baptizing them in the name of the Father and the Son and the Holy Spirit, teaching them to observe all that I commanded you; and lo, I am with you always, even to the end of the age."[36]

The early Christians took this mandate with the utmost seriousness. John Stott writes:

> The apostles also were controversialists, as is plain from the New Testament Epistles, and they appealed to their readers "to contend for the faith which was once for all delivered to the saints." Like their Lord and master they found it necessary to warn the churches of false teachers and urge them to stand firm in the truth.[37]

There are many examples of confrontation and controversy in the New Testament. For example, Paul had preached in a Jewish synagogue in Thessalonica, with the result that some had come to believe in the truth. However, those who opposed Paul formed a mob and incited a riot.[38] In this case, the mere preaching of the truth caused the confrontation. The apostles would hardly be described as men who had turned the world upside down[39] if they had soft-pedaled the truth. Truth and confrontation go hand in hand.

But here the problem arises: modern Christians have a dislike for dogmatism and a hatred of controversy. Both spring from a posture of accommodation to the thinking of this age. As noted, the present secular age does not at all accommodate itself to true Christianity.

And if the church is to confront the secular Goliath, it must not only have the willingness to engage in controversy, but also the proper mental equipment.

The Christian Mind

Controversy, it should be stressed, flows from the interaction of the truth with the falsehoods of the age. They should not result from the *manner* in which the truth is presented. In other words, in a confrontational situation, controversy should be a result of the *message*, not the messenger.

For example, when the Gospels note that the scribes and Pharisees were plotting to kill Jesus, they give the reason why: "For they were afraid of Him, for all the multitude was astonished at his *teaching*."[40]

Likewise, when Paul was in Athens, he was distressed

at the idolatry he saw. However, he did not rant and rave, nor simply harangue the Athenians about their sins and pagan religions, but rather he "reasoned" in the synagogue, "disputed" with the philosophers, and calmly addressd a meeting of the Aereopagus.[41] In other words, he was able to *argue* effectively, because he spoke the truth, and because he knew the minds of the listeners. He even quoted their own poets to them.[42] Some of the Athenians ridiculed him, but others found his message challenging and asked that he speak again. Had he attempted to forcibly indoctrinate them, it is doubtful whether they would have given him a hearing at all.

True Christianity, it should again be emphasized, speaks to all of life, not just to narrowly "religious" concerns. The comprehensive nature of the truth characteristic of the early apostles, especially Paul, must be restored. This is a problem of belief, to be sure, but also one of institutions.

Far from constituting an alternative to the diminishing academic and intellectual standards of public education, seminaries and Christian colleges have likewise become soft. In some cases they are places where ideas discarded by the nation's elite—ideas often hostile to Christianity, such as Marxism and Freudianism—may not only be taken seriously, but enjoy a long afterlife. In some cases, an attempt is made to integrate them with the Christian faith.

It may be that those who would minister effectively to their generation may have to seek their education in the best so-called "secular" schools, where there are rigorous standards, review by one's peers and so on. The specifically Christian seminaries and Bible colleges must come out of the spiritual ghetto. They must become institutions capable of equipping Christians for the intellectual combat that is part and parcel of confronting the world with the truth. Because of the sad state of Christian institutions, this will be quite difficult. But then, anything worthwhile is usually difficult. It was C. S. Lewis who noted that Christianity had not been tried and found wanting, but rather found difficult and not tried.

Internality-Externality

Here I would like to bring in my own experience. I was converted from agnosticism to Christianity in 1974. In the first six months of my Christian experience, I trekked from church to church—Baptist, Methodist, Presbyterian, Pentecostal—seeking a coherent whole in terms of my new-found faith. While I found myself struck by the "other-worldliness" of some of the activities, I also found a one-dimensional view of spiritual reality, the idea that the church building was the center of the religious experience and Christian duty. There is, of course, a sense in which this is true, but it seemed to me that the church should not hoard the truth within four walls. I was now a believer, but was I to just attend church services? Or was there something more?

It is true that Christianity is essentially internal. As a man thinks in his heart, so is he; if a man commits adultery in his heart, he is considered an adulterer. Christianity is also internal because the Holy Spirit inhabits the believer. However, this spiritual energy is for an external purpose, to create a righteous and fruitful life that the world can *see* and *experience*, just as they experience Jesus Christ Himself. In like manner, the true believer reflects the righteousness of God.

Christ said that believers are to love God with their entire being.[43] But how does the believer love God? It is not the unctuous, emotional product that many modern evangelicals associate with love. Rather, it is obedience. "If you love Me," says Christ, "you will keep My commandments."[44] Hence, love is both internal and external; it is right living according to the principles of the Bible.

Believers are to love their neighbors as they love themselves.[45] It cannot be denied that self-love permeates all of society, Christian and non-Christian. It can range from the athlete who exalts in the skill that has brought him victory to the institutions and monuments that Christians build and name after themselves.

Christ drew on this self-love and commanded the believer to treat others with equal amounts of love, care, and compassion. This is perhaps the clearest example of externality. Suffice it to say that a Christian experience that is only internal stands against human experience and reason. It also stands against the authority of the Bible.

Salt and Light

At one point Christ said:

> You are the salt of the earth; but if the salt has become tasteless, how will it be made salty again? It is good for nothing any more, except to be thrown out and trampled under foot by men.[46]

In Christ's time, salt was a preservative, used primarily to cure meats. In like manner, believers are to preserve and to cure. They are to preach and teach the gospel, the good news of Christ's atoning death and resurrection. In turn, this will have a curing and preserving effect on those who hear it, and on society as a whole. It is very much an "external" idea.

So is the concept of light. As Jesus also noted:

> You are the light of the world. A city set on a hill cannot be hidden. Nor do men light a lamp, and put it under the peck-measure, but on the lampstand; and it gives light to all who are in the house. Let your light shine before men in such a way that they may see your good works, and glorify your Father who is in heaven.[47]

A purely internal experience would be tantamount to putting one's light under a basket. In a properly externalized experience, it shines out like a beacon.

By serving as salt and light, true Christianity can be a corrective influence on society and the dominant culture. This will mean that more people will have a chance to hear the gospel. It is also the only way to preserve societal foundations from crumbling, and evil from running rampant.

Once after I spoke on salt and light principles, a woman approached me and stridently informed me that I was a radical. This was some time ago, and I did not know quite how to take it. I was new in the faith and simply believed what I was saying to be basic Biblical principles. Just what was a "radical"? As it happens, the root of the word radical is the Latin *radix*, meaning "root" or, by extension, "fundamental."[48]

In reality, then, a radical is someone who teaches fundamental principles that are the root and foundation of truth. I am not preaching rebellion or revolution, but simply stating that radicalism means that Christians should stand by the truth. It also means increased visibility for Christians. The great need is for a brand of radicalism that will seek out and challenge the secular mindset on every point.

Activism

We will now deal with what has been called "activism" or "social activism," normally defined as "a doctrine or practice that emphasizes direct vigorous action (as a mass demonstration) in support of or in opposition to one side of a controversial issue."[49] To what extent is this a legitimate activity for a Christian believer?

We have stressed that the primary task to which the believer is called is the preaching of the gospel and the living of a righteous life. In the Bible there are no commands to specific "social action" other than speaking and acting on the truth. But it seems clear that by doing that, the believer can have an influence on the world. Indeed he must be a "social activist" if he is faithful to God.

It should be added that activism is not necessarily "humanistic." There is a sense in which all people are humanists, that is, insofar as they believe in or practice humanitarianism. But a "humanist," strictly speaking, is one whose belief system and activism deliberately excludes God and has no transcendent reference point.

The activism of Christians flows from a sense of loving care for what God has created. The Christian has a responsibility to preserve both freedom and order, while keeping in mind his spiritual priorities and the limitations of the political process.

The Least of These
While Christians in the West generally have things easy—perhaps too easy—their brethren in the Communist bloc and various authoritarian regimes are suffering for their faith. There are countless stories of how Communist officials turn hungry rats on Christians in an effort to elicit a renunciation of faith; of Christians being sexually terrorized and sent to the Gulag for giving a Bible to a child. All this because they have dared to stand for the truth.[50]

Jesus Christ made it clear that those who perpetrate these atrocities are actually doing it to Him.

> " 'For I was hungry, and you gave Me something to eat; I was thirsty, and you gave Me drink; I was a stranger, and you invited Me in; naked, and you clothed Me; I was sick, and you visited Me; I was in prison, and you came to Me.' Then the righteous will answer Him, saying, 'Lord, when did we see You hungry, and feed You, or thirsty, and give You drink? And when did we see You a stranger, and invite You in, or naked, and clothe You? And when did we see You sick, or in prison, and come to You?' And the King will answer and say to them, 'Truly I say to you, to the extent that you did it to one of these brothers of Mine, even the least of them, you did it to Me.' "[51]

The New Testament is clear that we are to remember prisoners "as though in prison with them; and those who are ill-treated, since you yourselves are also in the body."[52] But what can be done?

First, believers must be in continual prayer for the

oppressed. When I speak to Christian audiences, I often ask those who pray for the oppressed in authoritarian states to raise their hands. In an audience of ten thousand, perhaps ten people usually do so. This is shameful. It goes without saying that the prayers offered on behalf of the oppressed should be fervent and specific, not general and vague. They should be aimed at gaining freedom for those who suffer.

Second, believers must financially support organizations that are smuggling Bibles and other materials into these countries. This could include the work of Brother Andrew and others.

Third, believers need to be missionaries, visiting and speaking with Christians behind the Iron Curtain. Attorneys should make themselves available to defend them, and Christians should contribute to this legal aid.

Fourth, believers should work at every level to undermine totalitarian governments. Unfortunately, America has not only failed to do this, but in some cases helps keep totalitarian states in the business of persecution and tyranny.

In short, believers should speak loudly and clearly on behalf of the oppressed, using every means at their disposal. They might take an example from the American Jewish community, which is quite vocal in its activism, and often effective in getting Jewish dissidents released. But if believers fail in this vital area, those oppressed will continue to languish in dungeons.

The Poor and Homeless
In the book of Proverbs, we find that the believer is commanded:

Open your mouth for the dumb, for the rights of all the
unfortunate. Open your mouth, judge righteously, and defend the rights of the afflicted and needy.[53]

There is a sense, then, in which activism—though not
necessarily the high-profile sort—is not an option for the
Christian. In fact, according to the New Testament, it has
much to do with true religion:

This is pure and undefiled religion in the sight of our God
and Father, to visit orphans and widows in their distress, and
to keep oneself unstained by the world.[54]

Activism may well be a synonym for what the Bible
calls good works. For example, the Bible strongly admon-
ishes Christians to be concerned about the poor. They are
to

Vindicate the weak and fatherless; do justice to the afflicted
and destitute. Rescue the weak and needy; deliver them out
of the hand of the wicked.[55]

One notes that, while Christians sometimes criticize
"homeless" advocates such as Mitch Snyder, they do little
to alleviate the problem themselves. There are, of course,
many organizations that are addressing poverty and home-
lessness. However, some of these have too much of their
resources invested in buildings, salaries and equipment, and
are hence sometimes limited in their effectiveness. There is
no one true way to address this problem, but true Christian
activism will at least not hesitate to get involved and to get
its hands dirty. It will not rely on organizations to do the
job.

The Role of the Gardener

One might consider the Christian's role to be that of a gardener, largely occupied with the pulling of weeds. Without this corrective action, the weeds will leach the vital nutrients and starve the fruit-bearing plants. One particularly dangerous weed, as we have noted, is the devaluation of human life, specifically in abortion.

Abortion

Abortion cuts to the heart of the sanctity of human life. It is *the* priority issue which believers should be actively resisting. Abortion is the spilling of innocent blood, and the Bible is quite clear as to the believer's responsibility in such cases:

> Deliver those who are being taken away to death, and those who are staggering to slaughter, O hold them back. If you say, "See, we did not know this," does He not consider it who weighs the hearts? And does He not know it who keeps your soul? And will He not render to every man according to his works?[56]

To paraphrase these verses, God commands the believer to take corrective action when innocent blood is spilled. Inaction on the part of an individual will lead to judgment of that person. Inaction on the part of a nation will bring judgment to that nation.

Because the sanctity of life is a cardinal doctrine of Christianity, abortion is therefore a theological issue. To God life is sacred. Therefore, the taking of innocent human life (since people are created in God's image and thus have great worth and dignity) is an attack against God as well as people. As such, there will be times when it is correct to break fellowship with other Christians over this issue. It is that high on the scale of priorities.

If those who say abortion is murder really believe it, they will do something about it. If every local church that claimed to believe the Bible joined together against abortion, it could be stopped. The fact that these churches have taken little or no action against abortion is a harbinger of justice and condemnation on them. Surely, if someone witnessed his father or mother being dragged off to a euthanasia clinic, he would act in a radical manner. The same principle applies to abortion.

What Is to Be Done?

There is no shortage of rhetoric surrounding the issue of abortion. But it is time to stop talking and start taking action. Many believers have worked with crisis pregnancy centers to stop abortions. These counsel pregnant women, with the result that many have both rejected abortion and become Christian believers themselves.

Instead of taking out larger mortgages to build larger church buildings, some local churches have helped start adoption agencies. Others have simply helped with adoptions so women can have their babies and put them up for adoption instead of killing them.

Many believers have been picketing abortion clinics, an effective method that abortionists fear. Picketing makes public something that all abortionists do not want people to know—that abortion is murder. Abortion is also big business, and since many Americans hesitate to cross a picket line, this activity also causes abortuaries considerable financial losses. Sometimes women receive effective counseling at the picket line and decide not to abort their child.

Picketing is a legal and effective method of social protest if done within certain defined parameters.[57] Some abortion clinics have moved into high-rise buildings in an attempt to avoid picketing. Others have filed lawsuits to stop the protesters, but the right to picket has generally been upheld.

Other believers, acting on the basis of conscience, have decided that nonviolent civil disobedience is the way God would have them oppose abortion. These use methods such as sit-ins to bring the issue of abortion to public light. However, if one is willing to break the law that person must also be willing to pay the price—that is, arrest, fines and often imprisonment.

Of course, violence is to be eschewed. Violence and physical attacks upon persons and destruction of property should *not* be condoned and practiced by those seeking change in free societies. Instead, violence and all unrestrained abuses should be condemned.

The Importance of Foundations

The radical counterculture movement of the 1960s and early 1970s, and the activism associated with it, has long since departed. In the mid-1970s, there was much activism for the cause of Christian schools. Ministers staged sit-ins or even chained themselves to pulpits to protest state intrusions.

However, today the Christian school movement does not take so many strong public stands and in some cases has shown itself more willing to submit to state regulation. Its earlier activism has been usurped by the home school movement, which may be perceived as an outgrowth of the failure of Christian schools to maintain their stand and provide an alternative to statist, secularized education.

One also notices that although abortion continues to be a powerful issue, the momentum of the anti-abortion forces seems to have peaked in the early 1980s.

The American system shows an astonishing ability to absorb all movements and co-opt even their most radical leaders. This happens when such movements become immersed in the politics of their cause, as opposed to first principles. The sometimes frenzied schedule of activists can cause individual burnout. And burnout is inevitable for an ideological movement with weak foundations.

The truth is, there are no "mass" movements; at best, a dedicated minority is involved. If it is to endure, any true activist movement must be based on a strong and enduring foundation. For example, anti-abortion activism must be based on the sanctity of life. In addition, any true activist movement must—as Christ did—originate and remain outside the establishment or status quo. It must eschew the belief that politics is the answer, and avoid the many groups that exploit the issues to raise money for their "nonprofit" organizations. It must not become absorbed in its own activism as an end in itself, but keep the goal in sight.

On an issue such as abortion, it will of course take more than either activism or politics to turn the tide. It will take a cultural revolution. How best to bring this about? Such a development can only take place through a change of *belief* on the part of the populace.

Hence those in the church should reject both a false pietism and a self-absorbed activism and dedicate themselves to the propagation of the truth and dedication to God on one hand, and the service of their fellows on the other hand. With this order of priorities, which maintains a strong spiritual and philosophical base, true activism can receive regular infusions of spiritual and ethical fuel. Only in this way can Christians be prepared for future crises. And if present trends are any indication, abortion is child's play compared to what's coming down the pike.

The Family

If Christians are to consistently speak and stand for the truth, it will be due not only to core beliefs, but also to a strong, undergirding family structure. This too is a foundation from which one can speak and act.

Historically and Biblically, the family is the central institution in society, with obvious procreative functions. Ideally, men and women marry because they share a bond of faith and love, and resolve to maintain this bond for life under God. They thus create a family system that cannot be duplicated by either science or imagination as the ideal institution for raising children.

There are many reasons why the family is the foundational institution of a free society.[58] First and foremost, it is the basic health and welfare institution, caring for and educating its own without any outside compulsion. As noted, when the family begins to break down, the state assumes the basic health, welfare and education functions and generally does an ineffective job. And there is no possibility that the state can fully replace the parents; hence, its performance will always be deficient.

The family is a person's first school and the parents are the educators, performing the most difficult of all educational tasks, teaching the child to speak. This is a difficult and painstaking task, but it comes simply and naturally in the family as an expression of the mother's love and the child's response to that love.

Moreover, as part of its educational function, the family is the government in the life of the child. Here children should learn self-government, motivation and guidance. Again, this flows naturally from the parents' love for their own. The children thus receive the highest order of motivation.

In a Biblically structured family, the father will serve as the head of the household. He is the authority within the family relationship. He should not, however, be a dictator.[59] Children are not the only ones who learn from, and are governed by, the family.

The mother is governed in her activities by the requirements of her husband and children. The father is governed by the necessities of providing for the family, protecting family members, and giving them the example and leadership they need. Conversely, a father who will not provide for his family will not be respected and will have neither the authority nor the ability to govern with wisdom and honor. The Bible states clearly that if anyone does not provide for his own, especially those of his own household, "he has denied the faith, and is worse than an unbeliever."[60]

Other Biblical injunctions deal with a current problem in the church. Many Christian men, unfortunately, imprison their wives in the house and treat them like slaves. This runs counter to the high estate placed upon women in the Bible and, in particular, to the reverent relationship men are to have toward women.

The husband is to love his wife "just as Christ loved the

church and gave Himself up for her."[61] Men are also to love their wives, "as their own bodies."[62] Failure to do so will interfere with God's blessing on that family.

Hence, Christian men need to shed their arrogant, macho posturings and help their wives, even if it means staying home and performing tasks normally thought of as "wifely" functions. Christ set the example by washing the feet of His disciples. In view of Christ's great sacrifice, surely the Christian husband can humble himself and love his wife. To do less is simply wrong.

However, another force that detracts from the family unit is the working mother of small children. This is not to say that women should not be in the workforce and treated equally in terms of wages and skills. It is simply to say that the years from birth through age five are a special time of nurture for young children, and that such children need their mothers to be with them. Psychological research bears this out.[63]

If at all possible, mothers should stay home with their young children, even if it hurts financially, and even if it means giving up that second car or otherwise dethroning the god of materialism.

As noted, both fathers and mothers who are workaholics are not good parents. This applies even if the causes that drive them are legitimate, or even if they are church activities. Parents must keep themselves within the family environment. They must also spend time with their children on a continuous basis, and keep them away from extracurricular activities that tend to disrupt families. Again, in some cases, these can be church activities. The family, in short, should be a living unit, not an atomized group of individuals.

The Television Trap

One practically universal intruder that prevents this kind of family unity is television. Many television programs and commercials are highly destructive for young minds. They eschew moral judgments and program viewers to buy products. In the realm of the commercial, nothing is sacred, which is evident in ads depicting computers dropping out of the sky to waiting monks, and executives posing as angelic beings, walking through clouds publicizing their products.

I must add that I am not completely anti-television. In our family, however, we place severe restrictions on our viewing and screen what our children watch. We have found that the best way to watch television is as a family, which allows both parental critique and interplay with the children in discussing the content. What we do not allow is television to serve as a baby-sitter. Intentional or not, television is a teacher, and if not controlled, a teacher of the worst sort.

Creativity and Interaction

I noted earlier the rather dismal state of Christian endeavors in the arts, how the Biblical and traditional view of the arts and creativity as gifts of God has largely been discarded.

Christians must emerge from their ghettos and acquire an ability to understand and discuss the arts intelligently. This does not mean that they are absorbed with the respective works or subjects, nor does it mean that the Christian necessarily approves of the content. It simply means that he or she should be able to interpret them in terms of their ideas and underlying ethos, and respond in the appropriate way. The arts, after all, often indicate the direction in which a society is heading. Picasso's painting, for example, effectively foretold an era of mass inhumanity.

Christians should disabuse themselves of the notion that all rock music is evil, or that all movies are evil. They must not be flippant condemners of everything and should be able to praise what is good, even if they do not agree with the lifestyle of the author or the content of the message. For example, one may not agree with the point of view of a particular film, but may still recognize merit in its technical aspects such as direction, cinematography, etc. (At the same time, however, one must, for example, be careful not to allow brilliant cinematography to seduce one into accepting an anti-Christian message.) One, moreover, may not be fond of jazz, but should be able to appreciate the skill of the musicians.

While all Christians should be able to interpret the arts, others will want to be participants. And there is no good reason why they should not do so. Indeed, there is every reason why they should. Artistic creativity is a gift of God. As such, it is the imagination of the Christian that should soar beyond the stars.[64] Just as the arts need no justification, Christian participation in them needs no justification. Involvement in the arts cannot be opposed on the grounds that the world is divided into "spiritual" and "secular" spheres. As it happens, the word *secular* does not appear in the Bible.

There is, however, an important caution. Those believers inclined to the arts must understand that their Christian faith and spirituality in themselves, however genuine and robust, offer them no guarantee of artistic brilliance or even general competence. Triumphalism is not only out of line, but can cause much embarrassment. In addition, the fact that someone is a well-known "Christian personality" may help them get a hearing, but, unfortunately, it does not insure that their artistic efforts will be of a high quality.

Whatever the Christian does, he or she is to do it as unto God. They must be satisfied with nothing less than the best. In practical terms, this means coming to grips with one's own abilities, or the lack of them, and settling down to a long and sometimes grueling apprenticeship. Simply put, art is difficult. Making a living as any kind of artist is more difficult still.

At present, there seems little good reason why the world should take Christian art seriously. Before they are to be heard or taken seriously in the artistic world Christians need to earn the *right* to be heard by developing their skill and artistic vision to the highest level. And in view of the present state of things, that is going to take quite a while.

The Mark of the Christian
To live a truly Christian life in a militantly secular age is a difficult and demanding task requiring all the measures we have hitherto outlined, and more. There is one element of true Christianity without which the most vibrant faith, the most fearless posture, the most brilliant apologetic, and even the most selfless service is incomplete. That element is love, which is not an option for the Christian.

When a lawyer asked Jesus which was the greatest commandment in the law, He replied that it was to love God with all your heart, soul, and mind, and to love your neighbor as yourself.[65] Jesus also said:

A new commandment I give to you, that you love one
another, even as I have loved you, that you also love one
another. By this all men will know that you are My disciples,
if you have love for one another.[66]

Given that this is a command, it follows that its violation is a sin. Francis Schaeffer wrote:

In the midst of the world, in the midst of our present
culture, Jesus is giving a right to the world. Upon His
authority He gives the world the right to judge whether you
and I are born-again Christians on the basis of our observable
love toward all Christians.[67]

In other words, if people challenge whether or not
believers are Christians because believers have not shown
love toward other Christians, it must be understood that
they are only exercising a prerogative which Christ gave
them. Also, as Schaeffer adds:

We must not get angry. If people say, "You don't love other
Christians," we must go home, get down on our knees, and
ask God whether or not they are right. And if they are, then
they have a right to have said what they said.[68]

In the midst of Christ's prayer in John 17:21, He prays
that "they may all be one; even as Thou, Father, art in Me,
and I in Thee, that they also may be in Us; that the world
may believe that Thou didst send Me." Here Jesus is pray-
ing for the oneness of the church among true Christians
who love one another.

Note the reason for this unity: "that the world may
believe that Thou didst send Me." This means that love is

the ultimate apologetic. We simply cannot expect the world to believe that the Father sent the Son unless the world sees the reality of Christ in believers.

A Definition of Love

To reflect their love for God, believers must love others as they love themselves. This love is effectively described and defined in 1 Corinthians 13:4-8:

> Love is patient, love is kind, and is not jealous; love does not brag and is not arrogant, does not act unbecomingly; it does not seek its own, is not provoked, does not take into account a wrong suffered, does not rejoice in unrighteousness, but rejoices with the truth; bears all things, believes all things, hopes all things, endures all things. Love never fails. . . .

Love, then, requires an "otherness," a focus away from oneself, a total respect for others as a way of reflecting Christ. This is the kind of expression and action that draws men toward the truth. It concerns what we may call "humanness." A primary task for this generation of believers is keeping humanness in the human race—that is, to upgrade and then maintain people's high place in the universe.

All people bear the image of God and have value, not simply because they happen to be redeemed, but because they are God's creation and made in God's image. Modern men and women who have rejected this truth have no clue as to why they exist or what their place in the universe is. Because of this, they often feel lost and find life absurd. Modern culture further downgrades and depersonalizes them. But the Christian believer should know the value of people as God's creation, and act out of that knowledge. All people are our neighbors. We are to love them as ourselves, even if they are unredeemed, and even if the cost of such loving is great.

Giving

In many ways, giving is the essence of love. C. S. Lewis noted:

> I am afraid the only safe rule is to give more than we can spare. In other words, if our expenditure on comforts, luxuries, amusements, etc., is up to the standard common among those with the same income as our own, we are probably giving away too little. If our charities do not at all pinch or hamper us, I should say they are too small. There ought to be things we should like to do and cannot do because our charitable expenditure excludes them.[69]

In other words, giving that is not sacrificial is not true giving. But giving is not limited to money or material items. It includes giving time to others, opening one's home to others and the general giving of oneself to serve others' needs. One example of this is Francis Schaeffer.

In his last year of life, Schaeffer was literally riddled with cancer. However, this did not cause him to stop lecturing. Sometimes he would have to stop and sit down for ten minutes or so, but then he would get up and finish the lecture. Not only so, but he would remain afterward to answer questions and discuss people's problems. This was his practice right up until the time he died. A similar spirit must prevail in believers if God is to be reflected in them.

Compassion

One place to start might be with those who need help the most. For example, why aren't American believers on the front line assisting the homeless? Christians should know that helping with physical needs is a prelude to meeting spiritual needs.

This is what true compassion is all about. It has nothing to do with weeping at tragedy, which might be more indicative of sentimentalism. Compassion is bringing justice to bear upon real-life situations.

However, true compassion often does have emotional accompaniment: outrage. Outrage is a legitimate reaction for Christians who see inhumanity. Unfortunately, the lack of outrage is a striking characteristic of modern Christianity, which allows some of the most heinous crimes in history—terrorism, abortion, oppression—to carry on before its very eyes.

Perhaps this happens because of lack of identification with the suffering of others. Identification, however, as Os Guinness notes, is at the heart of the Incarnation:

> As God became man in Jesus, he was no . . . Pentagon chief, making quick flying inspections on the front line, but one who shared the foxholes, who knew the risks, who felt the enemy fire. No other God has wounds. It is because God identified so fully with us that we can know him and trust him.[70]

In view of Christ's example, it won't do for Christians to entertain themselves in million-dollar cathedrals while poverty and death reign a few blocks away.

Persecution

If it happens that Christians proceed in a manner consistent with true Christianity, they may not demand or expect to move from victory to victory. In a depraved culture that often rivals Sodom and Gomorrah, they should expect opposition of the most hostile sort, even persecution.

John the Baptist spoke out against corruption in the court of Herod, and his actions wound up costing him his life. Christians can expect the same or even worse treatment, and modern technology provides persecutors with a variety of new alternatives. And if American Christians find themselves in foreign lands, the persecution might be heightened by nationalistic prejudice against foreigners in general and Americans in particular.

As Americans we currently have it easy. We do not compare well with the early church, nor with those lonely but intrepid souls behind the Iron Curtain, persecuted simply because they are believers who will not be silenced. I have had American Christians tell me that they would not fight for their freedom to speak the truth because they might lose their jobs.

Then there is the excuse that if one stands for the truth it will offend people and the Christian will lose his or her "witness." This is a fundamental cop-out to avoid the hard task of standing tall. One may be hated for a true witness, but one cannot lose that witness for speaking the truth.

In the final analysis, persecution will follow any strong stand for God. One must be prepared. And above all, one must count the cost.

Suffering

Suffering may be considered not an optional but rather an essential aspect of true Christianity. Christ foretold that the true beliver would be hated.[71] And He specifically noted that suffering and persecution would follow:

In the world you have tribulation, but take courage; I have overcome the world.[72]

For the Christian, suffering is never meaningless. Christ uses suffering as a way to mature and perfect the believer. The Scripture states:

It was fitting for Him, for whom are all things, and through whom are all things, in bringing many sons to glory, to perfect the author of their salvation through sufferings.[73]

How then shall followers of Christ escape the need for a similar process?

Suffering is also a preparation of the Christian's eventual union with God. "Through many tribulations," writes the Apostle Paul, "we must enter the kingdom of God."[74]

Moreover, the Scriptures state that those who suffer for the sake of righteousness are "blessed"[75] and may keep on rejoicing[76] because of the prospect of eventual exultation with God.

Provision for Failure

Practicing true Christianity and living consistently as a believer is a difficult task which at times seems impossible. The believer is told to run the race of life "in such a way that you may win,"[77] but failure is a definite possibility. In fact, we all fail. This is the human dilemma; this is reality. None of us is capable of doing everything. However, Christ does not expect us to do everything, and has assured us that His yoke is easy and His burden is light. He promises to give us rest.[78] In short, there is no cause for despair or pessimism.

Reasons for Hope

Who would have thought that a ragtag band of converts from an obscure Roman colony could have changed the course of history? And yet, that is precisely what happened. The fact that they prevailed beyond all odds is an inspiration.

Because of the breakdown of Western society, the present situation is often compared to that faced by the early church. However, one can make a good case that modern times, especially with the explosion of new technologies, have more in common with the sixteenth-century world of the Reformation: social foment, religious corruption, an outburst of learning, a dissatisfied populace, and so on. As Os Guinness has written:

> This was the period between the Renaissance and the Reformation when there was protest and re-evaluation everywhere. Renaissance humanism with all its brilliance had burst on the West, bringing with it not only the highest in art but also unrest, chaos, violence and disruption.[79]

The Reformation confronted all that, and its institutional source was one person in an obscure school. Today Martin Luther would be considered an upstart and the University of Wittenberg would be shrugged off as an insignificant junior faculty, only fifteen years old, with a total complement of one hundred and whose professors were mostly in their twenties.

However, equipped with great spiritual and intellectual power, along with fervent devotion to Jesus Christ, those professors greatly affected the world around them as well as the world to come. They are evidence of the Biblical truth that with God, all things are possible, and that one need not despair.

More important, they show that the God of true Christianity is sovereign. He is the omnipotent Lord of history, the Alpha and the Omega, the beginning and the ending. He will ultimately prevail, and in that assurance is great peace and great joy.

AUTHOR'S AFTERWORD

*M*y hopes in writing this book were to speak my mind in terms of what I have seen in the Christianity practiced around me. I did not set out to be overly critical but strove to be as accurate as possible.

In titling this work *True Christianity,* I am not in any way trying to be audacious or arrogant. I am simply giving my opinion on what I believe to be important concepts and issues within the context of what is here termed "true Christianity."

There is so much confusion as to how believers should be conducting themselves and responding to the crises of the moment. This book is hopefully a contribution that will help clear up some of the befuddlement and open an intelligent debate on the material discussed in this book.

Finally, since it is not possible for me to cover every aspect of Christianity in these pages, I suggest further study of the great works on systematic theology and Christianity by the great writers and theologians of the past (many of whom are listed in the bibliography). This author finds such works both helpful and humbling, and the title of the present work in no way implies that this rather brief treatise compares to such works.

John W. Whitehead
Culpeper, Virginia
November 1988

NOTES

Part One: The Human Dilemma

1. Christopher Lasch, *The Culture of Narcissism: American Life in an Age of Diminishing Expectations* (New York: Warner Books, 1979), p. 28.
2. Malachi Martin, *Hostage to the Devil: The Possession and Exorcism of Five Living Americans* (New York: Reader's Digest Press, 1976), p. 6.
3. Harrison E. Salisbury, *Book of the Month Club News,* Midsummer, 1974, pp. 4, 5. See also Paul G. Humber, "Stalin's Brutal Faith," *Impact,* October 1987.
4. John Barron and Anthony Paul, *Murder of a Gentle Land* (New York: Reader's Digest Books, 1977). Though once thought by some to be wildly exaggerated, this volume has stood the test of time and may be understated. See also Arch Puddington, "Pol Pot in Retrospect," *Commentary,* April 1987, p. 50.
5. Quoted in Edward E. Ericson, Jr., "Solzhenitsyn—Voice from the Gulag," *Eternity,* October 1985, pp. 23, 24.
6. C. G. Jung, *Collected Works,* Vol. XI (Princeton: Princeton University Press, 1969), pp. 334-336.
7. *Ibid.*
8. See Christine Gorman, "A Balancing Act of Life and Death," *Time,* February 1, 1988, p. 49.
9. C. S. Lewis, *The Abolition of Man* (New York: Macmillan, 1947), pp. 89, 90.
10. Harvey Cox, *The Secular City* (New York: Macmillan, 1965).
11. "ACLU Blocks Lily Crosses," *Washington Post,* April 2, 1988, p. C11.
12. "Preachers Tried for Loud Speeches," *The Rutherford Institute Magazine,* November-December 1986, p. 5. See also *The Rutherford Institute Magazine,* October-December 1987, p. 21.

13. J. O. Wilson, *Public Schools of Washington,* Vol. I, Records of the Columbia Historical Society, 1897, p. 4.

14. *Ibid.,* p. 5.

15. *Ibid.,* p. 6.

16. See Terry Eastland, "In Defense of Religious America," *Commentary,* June 1981, p. 40.

17. The cases and others like them were handled by The Rutherford Institute, P.O. Box 510, Manassas, Virginia 22110.

18. "Student Sues After Seizure of Bibles," *The Rutherford Institute Magazine,* September-October 1985, p. 4; "School Board Erred in Seizing Bibles," *The Rutherford Institute Magazine,* September-October 1986, p. 17.

19. This author would agree that such material, especially about the Nazis, should in fact be displayed. It may prevent such things from happening again.

20. "Students Fight Censorship of Posters," *The Rutherford Institute Magazine,* September-October 1986, p. 21; "Court Strikes Down Censorship of Student's Speech," *The Rutherford Institute Magazine,* July-September 1987, p. 7.

21. "Censored Speech Provokes Lawsuit," *The Rutherford Institute Magazine,* October-December 1987, p. 4.

22. For a more detailed discussion and examples, see John W. Whitehead, *Parents' Rights* (Westchester, Ill.: Crossway Books, 1985).

23. Malcolm Muggeridge, *Christ and the Media* (Grand Rapids: Eerdmans, 1977), p. 23.

24. See Robert Lichter, Stanley Rothman, and Linda Lichter, *The Media Elite: America's New Powerbrokers* (Bethesda: Adler and Adler, 1986), p. 22.

Part Two: A False Faith

1. Michael Harrington, *The Politics at God's Funeral: The Spiritual Crisis of Western Civilization* (New York: Holt, Rinehart, Wilson, 1983), p. 165.

2. *Ibid.*

3. George Gallup Jr., *Forecast 2000: George Gallup Jr. Predicts the Future of America* (New York: William Morrow, 1984), p. 152.

4. *Ibid.,* p. 153.

5. Richard Lovelace, *Dynamics of Spiritual life: An Evangelical Theology of Renewal* (Downers Grove, Ill.: InterVarsity Press, 1979), p. 85.

6. Quoted in Malcolm Muggeridge, *Christ and the Media* (Grand Rapids: Eerdmans, 1977), p. 49.

7. C. S. Lewis, *God in the Dock: Essays on Theology and Ethics* (Grand Rapids: Eerdmans, 1971), p. 262.

8. Luke 15:1-2.

9. Luke 18:9-14.

10. Galatians 3:28, *New International Version.*

11. John 17:15.
12. John R. W. Stott, *Christ the Controversialist* (Downers Grove, Ill.: InterVarsity Press, 1970), p. 184.
13. *Ibid.,* p. 182.
14. Mark 13:32.
15. Stott, *Christ the Controversialist,* p. 188.
16. Erik Erikson, *Childhood and Society* (New York: Norton, 1963), pp. 79, 80.
17. Ephesians 6:12.
18. 2 Corinthians 10:4.
19. Neil Postman, *Amusing Ourselves to Death: Public Discourse in the Age of Show Business* (New York: Vantage Books, 1985), pp. 116, 117.
20. *Ibid.,* pp. 118, 119.
21. *Ibid.,* pp. 119, 120.
22. Muggeridge, *Christ and the Media,* p. 60.
23. *Ibid.,* p. 30.
24. *Ibid.,* pp. 23-42.
25. Postman, *Amusing Ourselves to Death,* p. 123.
26. Ben Armstrong, *The Electronic Church* (Nashville: Thomas Nelson, 1979), p. 137.
27. Postman, *Amusing Ourselves to Death,* p. 121.
28. *Ibid.,* p. 117.
29. *Ibid.,* pp. 187, 188.
30. Harry Blamires, *The Christian Mind* (Ann Arbor: Servant Books, 1978), p. 3.
31. Franky Schaeffer, *Addicted to Mediocrity* (Westchester, Ill.: Crossway Books, 1981), pp. 21, 23.
32. 1 Peter 4:17.

Part Three: True Christianity

1. Christopher Lasch, *The Culture of Narcissism: American Life in an Age of Diminishing Expectations* (New York: Warner Books, 1979), p. 28.
2. Quoted in Os Guinness, *The Dust of Death* (Downers Grove, Ill.: InterVarsity Press, 1973), p. 364.
3. Isaiah 6:8.
4. Richard F. Lovelace, *Dynamics of Spiritual Life: An Evangelical Theology of Renewal* (Downers Grove, Ill.: InterVarsity Press, 1979), p. 85.
5. Romans 1:4.
6. Acts 13:33.
7. 1 Corinthians 15:14.
8. 1 Corinthians 15:45.
9. 1 Corinthians 15:47.
10. Revelation 1:5.
11. Malcolm Muggeridge, *Christ and the Media* (Grand Rapids: Eerdmans, 1977), p. 71.
12. 1 Corinthians 13:12.

13. Ephesians 6:12.
14. John 8:32.
15. Galatians 2:20.
16. Galatians 5:22-23.
17. Matthew 4:3.
18. See Fyodor Dostoyevsky, *The Brothers Karamazov* (New York: Bantam Books, 1970), pp. 297-319.
19. Matthew 4:4.
20. Galatians 5:13-14.
21. Matthew 11:19.
22. Matthew 18:20.
23. See 1 Corinthians 12:13; also see Ephesians 4.
24. Romans 16:5.
25. 1 Corinthians 16:2; Acts 20:7.
26. Acts 6:1-6.
27. 1 Timothy 3:1-13; Titus 1:5-9.
28. Acts 15.
29. See Francis A. Schaeffer, *The Church at the End of the Twentieth Century* (Westchester, Ill.: Crossway Books, 1985), pp. 63-67.
30. *Ibid.*
31. 1 Timothy 3:15, *New International Version.*
32. Acts 21:39.
33. John R. W. Stott, *Christ the Controversialist* (Downers Grove, Ill.: InterVarsity Press, 1970), pp. 13, 14.
34. Matthew 21:12-13.
35. Mark 11:16.
36. Matthew 28:18-20.
37. John R. W. Stott, *Christ the Controversialist,* p. 18.
38. Acts 15:5.
39. Acts 17:6.
40. Mark 11:18 (emphasis supplied).
41. Acts 17:16-21.
42. Acts 17:28.
43. Matthew 22:37.
44. John 14:15.
45. Matthew 22:39.
46. Matthew 5:13.
47. Matthew 5:14-16.
48. See *Webster's New Collegiate Dictionary* (Springfield: G. And C. Merriam, 1975), pp. 951, 952.
49. *Ibid.,* p. 12.
50. See Richard Wurmbrand, *Tortured for Christ* (Glendale: Diane Books, 1967; Westchester, Ill.: Crossway Books, 1987).
51. Matthew 25:35-40.
52. Hebrews 13:3.
53. Proverbs 31:8-9.
54. James 1:27.

55. Psalm 82:3-4.
56. Proverbs 24:11-12.
57. See John W. Whitehead, *The Right to Picket and the Freedom of Public Discourse* (Westchester, Ill.: Crossway Books, 1984).
58. See Rousas John Rushdoony, *Law and Liberty* (Nutley, N.J.: Craig Press, 1971), pp. 78-81.
59. Ephesians 5:22-33; 6:1-4.
60. 1 Timothy 5:8.
61. Ephesians 5:25.
62. Ephesians 5:28.
63. See John W. Whitehead, *Parents' Rights* (Westchester, Ill.: Crossway Books, 1985).
64. See Francis A. Schaeffer, *Art and the Bible* (Downers Grove, Ill.: InterVarsity Press, 1973).
65. Matthew 22:35-40.
66. John 13:34-35.
67. Francis A. Schaeffer, *The Complete Works of Francis A. Schaeffer*, Vol. 4 (Westchester, Ill.: Crossway Books, 1982), p. 187.
68. *Ibid.,* pp. 187, 188.
69. C. S. Lewis, *Mere Christianity* (New York: Macmillan, 1943), pp. 81, 82.
70. Os Guinness, *The Dust of Death*, p. 187.
71. John 15:18.
72. John 16:33.
73. Hebrews 2:10.
74. Acts 14:22.
75. 1 Peter 3:14.
76. Matthew 5:12.
77. 1 Corinthians 9:24.
78. Matthew 11:28-29; Hebrews 4:9.
79. Os Guinness, *The Dust of Death*, p. 391.

SELECT BIBLIOGRAPHY

*A*s the heading suggests, this bibliography makes no pretense to be exhaustive. I have listed only the works I have actually used and cited in the text and/or referred to in the process of writing this book. Even so, for a subject as complex and multidimensional as set forth in the text, it is impossible to remember, let alone do full justice to, all the writings which have helped to form my opinion.

Ackroyd, Peter. *T. S. Eliot: A Life.* New York: Simon and Schuster, 1984.

"ACLU Blocks Lily Crosses." *Washington Post,* 2 April 1988, p. C11.

Ahlstrom, Sydney. *A Religious History of the American People.* New Haven: Yale University Press, 1972.

Anderson, J. N. D. *Christianity: The Witness of History.* Downers Grove, Ill.: InterVarsity, 1970.

Andrew, Brother. *The Ethics of Smuggling.* Wheaton, Ill.: Tyndale House, 1979.

Arendt, Hannah. *On Revolution.* New York: Viking Press, 1965.

Armstrong, Ben. *The Electronic Church.* Nashville: Thomas Nelson, 1979.

Augustine, St. *The City of God* (413-426). 2 vols. New York: Dutton, 1945.

Bainton, Roland. *The Travail of Religious Liberty.* Hamden, Conn.: Shoe String Press, 1971.

Barclay, William. *The Ten Commandments for Today.* Grand Rapids, Mich.: Eerdmans, 1977.

Barron, John and Paul, Anthony. *Murder of a Gentle Land.* New York: Reader's Digest Books, 1977.

Barth, Karl. *The Epistle to the Romans* (1919). New York: Oxford University Press, 1933.

————. *Preaching Through the Christian Year.* Grand Rapids, Mich.: Eerdmans, 1968.

Bass, Archer B. *Protestantism in the United States.* New York: Thomas Y. Crowell, 1929.

Blamires, Harry. *The Christian Mind.* Ann Arbor, Mich.: Servant Books, 1978.

————. *On Christian Truth.* Ann Arbor, Mich.: Servant Books, 1983.

Boorstin, Daniel. *Image; or, What Happened to the American Dream.* New York: Atheneum, 1962.

Borisov, Vadim. "Personality and National Awareness." *From Under the Rubble.* New York: Little, Brown, 1975.

Brown, Colin. *Philosophy and the Christian Faith.* Downers Grove, Ill.: InterVarsity, 1969.

Brown, Harold O. J. *Heresies.* Garden City, New York: Doubleday, 1984.

Bullock, Alan. *Hitler: A Study in Tyranny.* Rev. ed. New York: Harper and Row, 1962.

Burgess, Anthony. *The Clockwork Orange.* New York: Norton, 1963.

Calvin, John. *The Institutes of the Christian Religion.* 2 vols. (1536-1559). Reprint. Philadelphia: Westminster Press, 1960.

Carse, James. *Jonathan Edwards & The Visibility of God.* New York: Charles Scribner's Sons, 1967.

"Censored Speech Provokes Lawsuit." *The Rutherford Institute Magazine,* October-December 1987, p. 4.

Chabannes, Jacques. *Saint Augustine.* Garden City, N.Y.: Doubleday, 1962.

Chesterton, G. K. *Collected Works: Heretics, Orthodoxy, and Blatchford Controversies.* Vol. I. San Francisco: Ignatius Press, 1986.

Cohn, Norman. *The Pursuit of the Millennium.* New York: Oxford University Press, 1970.

Colson, Charles. *Kingdoms in Conflict.* New York and Grand Rapids, Mich.: William Morrow and Zondervan, 1987.

"Court Strikes Down Censorship of Student's Speech." *The Rutherford Institute Magazine,* July-September 1987, p. 7.

Cox, Harvey. *Religion in the Secular City: Toward a Postmodern Theology.* New York: Simon and Schuster, 1984.

Darwin, Charles. *The Origin of Species by Means of Natural Selection or the Preservation of Favoured Races in the Struggle for Life* (1859). New York: Oxford University Press, 1963.

Devlin, Patrick. *Enforcement of Morals.* London: Oxford University Press, 1959.

Dostoyevsky, Fyodor. *The Brothers Karamazov.* New York: Bantam Books, 1970.

Dreisbach, Daniel L. *Real Threat and Mere Shadow: Religious Liberty and The First Amendment.* Westchester, Ill.: Crossway Books, 1987.

Eastland, Terry. "In Defense of Religious America." *Commentary,* June 1981, p. 40.

Eddy, George Sherwood. *The Kingdom of God and the American Dream.* New York: Harper and Row, 1941.

Ellul, Jacques. *The Technological Society.* New York: Vintage Books, 1964.

———. *Living Faith: Belief and Doubt in a Perilous World.* New York: Harper and Row, 1983.

Ericson, Jr., Edward E. "Solzhenitsyn—Voice from the Gulag." *Eternity,* October 1985.

Erikson, Erik. *Childhood and Society.* New York: Norton, 1963.

Flake, Carol. *Redemptorama: Culture, Politics, and the New Evangelicalism.* New York: Anchor Press, 1984.

Fox, Robin Lane. *Pagans and Christians.* New York: Knopf, 1987.

Frend, W. H. C. *The Rise of Christianity.* Philadelphia: Fortress Press, 1984.

Freud, Sigmund. *Civilization and Its Discontents*. New York: Doubleday, 1958.

————. *The Future of an Illusion*. Garden City, N.Y.: Anchor Books, 1964.

————. *Moses and Monotheism*. New York: Knopf, 1949.

Fullerton, Kemper. *Calvinism and Capitalism*. *Harvard Theological Review*, July 1928.

Gallup, George, Jr. *Forecast 2000: George Gallup, Jr., Predicts the Future of America*. New York: William Morrow, 1984.

Gibbon, Edward. *The Decline and Fall of the Roman Empire* (1776-1788). 6 vols. Reprint. New York: Dutton, 1910.

Goddard, Donald. *The Last Days of Dietrich Bonhoeffer*. New York: Harper and Row, 1976.

Gorman, Christine. "A Balancing Act of Life and Death." *Time*, 1 February 1988.

Gorman, Michael J. *Abortion and the Early Church*. Downers Grove, Ill.: InterVarsity Press, 1982.

Gough, Michael. *The Origins of Christian Art*. New York: Praeger, 1973.

Greer, Germaine. *Sex and Destiny*. New York: Harper and Row, 1984.

Grimal, Pierre. *The Civilization of Rome*. New York: Simon and Schuster, 1963.

Gross, Bertram. *Friendly Fascism: The New Face of Power in America*. New York: M. Evans, 1980.

Guinness, Os. *The Dust of Death*. Downers Grove, Ill.: InterVarsity Press, 1973.

Hall, Thomas Cuming. *The Religious Background of American Culture*. Boston: Little, Brown, 1930.

Handy, Robert T. *A Christian America: Protestant Hopes and Historical Realities*. London: Oxford University Press, 1971.

Harrington, Michael. *The Politics at God's Funeral; The Spiritual Crisis of Western Civilization*. New York: Holt, Rinehart and Winston, 1983.

Hegel, Georg W. F. *The Logic of Hegel*. New York: Oxford University Press, 1982.

Heidegger, Martin. *Being and Time*. New York: Harper and Row, 1962.

Heimert, Alan, and Miller, Perry, eds. *The Great Awakening.* Indianapolis: Bobbs-Merrill, 1967.

Hill, Christopher. *The Century of Revolution (1703-1714).* New York: Nelson, 1961.

————. *Milton and the English Revolution.* New York: Viking Press, 1978.

Hillel, Marc, and Henry, Clarissa. *Of Pure Blood.* New York: McGraw-Hill, 1976.

Hillerbrand, Hans J. *The Protestant Reformation.* New York: Walker, 1968.

Hodge, A. A. *The Confession of Faith* (1869). Carlisle, Penn.: Banner of Truth Trust, 1958.

Hopkins, Charles Howard. *The Rise of the Social Gospel in American Protestantism, 1865-1915.* New Haven: Yale University Press, 1940.

Hudson, Winthrop S. *Religion in America.* New York: Charles Scribner's Sons, 1973.

Hughes, Phillip. *A History of the Church.* Vol. 2. New York: Sheed and Ward, 1949.

Humber, Paul G. "Stalin's Brutal Faith." *Impact,* October 1987.

Huxley, Aldous. *Brave New World.* New York: Bantam Books, 1968.

Jackson, Jeremy. *No Other Foundation.* Westchester, Ill.: Crossway Books, 1980.

Jaspers, Karl. *Man in the Modern Age.* New York: Doubleday, 1957.

Johnson, Alan F. *The Freedom Letter.* Chicago: Moody Press, 1974.

Johnson, Paul. *A History of Christianity.* New York: Atheneum, 1976.

————. *Modern Times: The World from the Twenties to the Eighties.* New York: Harper and Row, 1983.

Jung, C. G. *Collected Works.* Vol. II. Princeton, N.J.: Princeton University Press, 1969.

Kaufmann, Walter, trans. *The Portable Nietzsche.* New York: Viking Press, 1968.

Koch, H. W. *Hitler Youth: The Duped Generation.* New York: Ballantine Books, 1972.

Koestler, Arthur. *Darkness at Noon.* New York: Macmillan, 1941.

Kuehnelt-Leddihn, Erik von. *Leftism: From de Sade and Marx to Hitler and Marcuse.* New Rochelle, N.Y.: Arlington House, 1974.

Küng, Hans. *On Being A Christian.* Garden City, N.Y.: Doubleday, 1976.

Lasch, Christopher. *The Culture of Narcissism: American Life in an Age of Diminishing Expectations.* New York: Warner Books, 1979.

Laski, Harold, ed. *A Defense of Liberty Against Tyrants: A Translation of the "Vindiciae Contra Tyrranos."* Gloucester, Mass.: Peter Smith, 1963.

Latourette, Kenneth Scott. *A History of Christianity.* New York: Harper and Row, 1953.

Lewis, C. S. *Mere Christianity.* New York: Macmillan, 1943.

————. *The Great Divorce.* New York: Macmillan, 1946.

————. *The Abolition of Man.* New York: Macmillan, 1947.

————. *Miracles.* New York: Macmillan, 1947.

————. *The Screwtape Letters.* New York: Macmillan, 1959.

————. *The Problem of Pain.* New York: Macmillan, 1962.

————. *The Discarded Image.* New York: Cambridge University Press, 1964.

————. *God in the Dock: Essays on Theology and Ethics.* Grand Rapids, Mich.: Eerdmans, 1971.

Lichter, Robert and Rothman, Stanley and Lichter, Linda. *The Media Elite: America's New Powerbrokers.* Bethesda, Md.: Adler and Adler, 1986.

Locke, John. *On the Reasonableness of Christianity* (1695). Chicago: Henry Regnery, 1965.

Lovelace, Richard. *Dynamics of Spiritual Life: An Evangelical Theology of Renewal.* Downers Grove, Ill.: InterVarsity Press, 1979.

Luther, Martin. *Ninety-Five Theses* (1517). Philadelphia: Fortress, 1957.

————. *Works of Martin Luther.* 6 Vols. Grand Rapids, Mich.: Baker Book House, 1982.

Machen, J. Gresham. *The Origin of Paul's Religion.* Grand Rapids, Mich.: Eerdmans, 1925.

————. *The Christian Faith in the Modern World*. Grand Rapids, Mich.: Eerdmans, 1965.

Mackay, Charles. *Extraordinary Popular Delusions and the Madness of Crowds* (1841). New York: Farrar, Straus and Giroux, 1932.

MacMullen, Ramsay. *Christianizing the Roman Empire (A.D. 100-400)*. New Haven: Yale University Press, 1984.

Mannix, Daniel P. *Those About to Die*. New York: Ballantine Books, 1958.

Marcuse, Herbert. *One Dimensional Man*. Boston: Beacon Press, 1964.

Marius, Richard. *Luther: A Biography*. Philadelphia: J. P. Lippincott, 1974.

Martin, Malachi. *Hostage to the Devil: The Possession and Exorcism of Five Living Americans*. New York: Reader's Digest Press, 1976.

Marty, Martin E. *Modern American Religion: The Irony of It All, 1893-1919*. Vol. I. Chicago: University of Chicago Press, 1986.

Marx, Karl and Engels, Friedrich. *The Manifesto of the Communist Party* (1848). San Francisco, Calif.: China Books, 1965.

McLuhan, Marshall. *Understanding Media*. New York: Mentor Books, 1964.

————. "Cybernation and Culture." *The Social Impact of Cybernetics*. New York: Simon and Schuster, 1966.

Meeks, Wayne A. *The First Urban Christians: The Social World of the Apostle Paul*. New Haven: Yale University Press, 1983.

————. *The Moral World of the First Christians*. Philadelphia: Westminster Press, 1986.

Middlemann, Udo. *Pro-Existence*. Downers Grove, Ill.: Inter-Varsity Press, 1974.

Miller, Perry. *The Life of the Mind in America*. London: Victor Gallancz, 1966.

Morris, Henry M. and John Whitcomb. *The Genesis Flood*. Philadelphia: Presbyterian and Reformed, 1961.

Morris, Leon. *The Apostolic Preaching of the Cross*. Grand Rapids, Mich.: Eerdmans, 1955.

Muggeridge, Malcolm. *Jesus Rediscovered.* Garden City, N.Y.: Doubleday, 1969.

————. *Jesus: The Man Who Lives.* New York: Harper and Row, 1975.

————. *Christ and the Media.* Grand Rapids, Mich.: Eerdmans, 1977.

Nathanson, Bernard N. *Aborting America.* Garden City, N.Y.: Doubleday, 1979.

Neuhaus, Richard J. *The Naked Public Square: Religion & Democracy in America.* Grand Rapids, Mich.: Eerdmans, 1984.

Orwell, George. *Animal Farm.* New York: New American Library, 1963.

Perry, Ralph Barton. *Puritanism and Democracy.* New York: Vanguard Press, 1944.

Phillips, Kevin P. *Post-Conservative America: People, Politics, and Ideology in a Time of Crisis.* New York: Random House, 1982.

Pink, Arthur W. *Eternal Security.* Grand Rapids, Mich.: Guardian Press, 1974.

Pit, Jan. *Persecution: It Will Never Happen Here?* Orange, Calif.: Open Doors, 1981.

Postman, Neil. *Amusing Ourselves to Death: Public Discourse in the Age of Show Business.* New York: Vantage Books, 1985.

"Preachers Tried for Loud Speeches." *The Rutherford Institute Magazine,* November-December 1986, p. 5.

Puddington, Arch. "Pol Pot in Retrospect." *Commentary,* April 1987.

Reichley, A. James. *Religion in American Public Life.* Washington, D.C.: The Brookings Institution, 1985.

Reincourt, Amaury de. *The Coming Caesars.* New York: Coward-McCann, 1957.

Revel, Jean-Francois. *The Totalitarian Temptation.* Garden City, N.Y.: Doubleday, 1977.

————. *How Democracies Perish.* Garden City, N.Y.: Doubleday, 1983.

Rookmaaker, H. R. *Modern Art and the Death of a Culture.* Downers Grove, Ill.: InterVarsity Press, 1970.

Rosenstock-Huessy, Eugen. *The Christian Future: Or the Mod-*

ern Mind Outrun. New York. Harper and Row, 1966.

Rosten, Leo, ed. *Religions of America.* New York: Simon and Schuster, 1975.

Runciman, Steven. *The First Crusade.* Cambridge: Cambridge University Press, 1980.

Rushdoony, Rousas John. *Law and Liberty.* Nutley, N.J.: Craig Press, 1971.

_____. *The Institutes of Biblical Law.* Nutley, N.J.: Craig Press, 1973.

_____. *Freud.* Philadelphia: Presbyterian and Reformed, 1975.

_____. *The Messianic Character of American Education.* Nutley, N.J.: Craig Press, 1976.

Russell, Bertrand. *Why I Am Not a Christian.* New York: Simon and Schuster, 1957.

Salisbury, Harrison E. *Book of the Month Club News.* Midsummer 1974, pp. 4, 5.

Schaeffer, Edith. *What Is a Family?* Old Tappan, N.J.: Revell, 1975.

Schaeffer, Francis A. *The Complete Works of Francis A. Schaeffer: A Christian WorldView.* Westchester, Ill.: Crossway Books, 1982.

_____. *The Great Evangelical Disaster.* Westchester, Ill.: Crossway Books, 1984.

Schaeffer, Franky. *Addicted to Mediocrity.* Westchester, Ill.: Crossway Books, 1981.

_____. *A Time for Anger: The Myth of Neutrality.* Westchester, Ill.: Crossway Books, 1982.

_____. *Bad News for Modern Man.* Westchester, Ill.: Crossway Books, 1984.

Schaeffer, Franky, and Harold Fickett. *A Modest Proposal for Peace, Prosperity and Happiness.* Nashville, Tenn.: Thomas Nelson, 1985.

"School Board Erred in Seizing Bibles." *The Rutherford Institute Magazine,* September-October 1986, p. 17.

Shirer, William L. *The Rise and Fall of the Third Reich: A History of Nazi Germany.* New York: Simon and Schuster, 1960.

Sire, James W. *The Universe Next Door.* Downers Grove, Ill.:

InterVarsity Press, 1976.

Skinner, B. F. *Beyond Freedom and Dignity.* New York: Knopf, 1971.

Solzhenitsyn, Aleksandr I. *August, 1914.* New York: Farrar, Straus and Giroux, 1972.

―――. *The Gulag Archipelago* (1918-1956). New York: Harper and Row, 1973.

―――. *Letter to the Soviet Leaders.* New York: Harper and Row, 1974.

―――. *The Gulag Archipelago* (1918-1956) (Two). New York: Harper and Row, 1975.

―――. *Lenin in Zurich.* New York: Farrar, Straus and Giroux, 1976.

―――. *The Gulag Archipelago* (1918-1956) (Three). New York: Harper and Row, 1978.

―――. *The Oak and the Calf.* New York: Harper and Row, 1980.

Spengler, Oswald. *The Decline of the West* (1918-1922). 2 vols. New York: Knopf, 1945.

Spurgeon, C. H. *The Cheque-Book of the Bank of Faith.* Pasadena, Tex.: Pilgrim Publications, 1975.

Stauffer, Ethelbert. *Christ and the Caesars.* Philadelphia: Westminster Press, 1965.

Stott, John R. W. *Christ the Controversialist.* Downers Grove, Ill.: InterVarsity Press, 1970.

Stout, Cushing. *The New Heavens and New Earth: Political Religion in America.* New York: Harper and Row, 1974.

Stout, Harry S. *The New England Soul: Preaching and Religious Culture in Colonial New England.* New York: Oxford University Press, 1986.

"Students Fight Censorship of Posters." *The Rutherford Institute Magazine,* September-October 1986, p. 21.

"Student Sues After Seizure of Bibles." *The Rutherford Institute Magazine,* September-October 1985, p. 4.

Tenney, Merrill C. *John: The Gospel of Belief.* Grand Rapids, Mich.: Eerdmans, 1948.

Terry, Maury. *The Ultimate Evil: An Investigation of America's Most Dangerous Satanic Cult.* Garden City, N.Y.: Doubleday, 1987.

Thomas, Cal. *The Death of Ethics in America.* Waco, Texas: Word Books, 1988.

Teilhard de Chardin, Pierre. *The Phenomenon of Man.* New York: Harper and Row, 1959.

Tillich, Paul. *Dynamics of Faith.* New York: Harper and Row, 1957.

————. *Systematic Theology.* 3 vols. Chicago: University of Chicago Press, 1967.

Tocqueville, Alexis de. *Democracy in America* (1835-1840). Vol. I. New York: Vintage Books, 1954.

Toffler, Alvin. *The Third Wave.* New York: Bantam Books, 1981.

Tucker, Robert C., ed. *The Marx-Engels Reader.* New York: W. W. Norton, 1978.

Tuveson, Ernest. *Redeemer Nation: The Idea of America's Millennial Role.* Chicago: University of Chicago Press, 1968.

Vitz, Paul C. *Psychology as Religion: The Cult of Self-Worship.* Grand Rapids, Mich.: Eerdmans, 1977.

Walzer, Michael. *Exodus and Revolution.* New York: Basic Books, 1985.

Wilson, J. O. *Public Schools of Washington.* Vol. I, Records of the Columbia Historical Society, 1897.

Woodward, Bob and Armstrong, Scott. *The Brethren: Inside the Supreme Court.* New York: Simon and Schuster, 1979.

Wurmbrand, Richard. *Tortured for Christ.* Glendale, Calif.: Diane Books, 1967; Westchester, Ill.: Crossway Books, 1987.

INDEX